MUSIC
IN
GENERAL
EDUCATION

Edited by

Karl D. Ernst and Charles L. Gary

MUSIC EDUCATORS NATIONAL CONFERENCE

1201 Sixteenth Street, N.W.   Washington, D.C. 20036

Printed in U. S. A.

MENC Committee on Music in General Education

Karl D. Ernst, *Chairman*
Chairman, Division of Creative Arts
California State College at Hayward
Hayward, California

Charles H. Benner
Assistant Professor of Music Education
The Ohio State University
Columbus, Ohio

Frank L. D'Andrea
Chairman, Music Department
Western Washington State College
Bellingham, Washington

Charles L. Gary
Associate Executive Secretary
Music Educators National Conference
Washington, D. C.

William C. Hartshorn
Supervisor in Charge, Music Education
Los Angeles City Schools
Los Angeles, California

William M. Lamers
Assistant Superintendent
Milwaukee Public Schools
Milwaukee, Wisconsin

Emile H. Serposs
Director of Music Education
Chicago Public Schools
Chicago, Illinois

Chester C. Travelstead
Dean, College of Education
University of New Mexico
Albuquerque, New Mexico

Louis G. Wersen
Director, Division of Music Education
Philadelphia Public Schools
Philadelphia, Pennsylvania

David L. Wilmot
Associate Professor of Music
University of Florida
Gainesville, Florida

iii

Preface

ONE of the outstanding achievements of public school music during the present century has been the phenomenal development of performance groups. At the secondary level, these groups have often reached an astounding level of perfection. As the performance program grew in importance and was accepted by the public, the training of the secondary school music teacher became increasingly dominated by courses which were directly related to a performance oriented music curriculum.

In more recent years, however, graduate students and other thoughtful music educators began to evaluate the outcomes of music education, and they expressed increasing concern with the fact that in spite of the high standards of performance in many schools, the large majority of high school students had no formal contact with music during any of their high school years. They also noted that even those students who were active in performance groups, though technically well trained, were frequently deficient in understanding music as an art.

During the first Interim Leadership Meeting sponsored by the Music Educators National Conference and held at Interlochen, Michigan in August of 1959, there was a strong recommendation by the state and national leaders who were in attendance that the MENC should engage in a vigorous study of this entire problem and develop an appropriate publication.

As a first step a survey of practices was conducted through the pages of the Music Educators Journal and in cooperation with affiliated state music education organizations. Then a committee was appointed and charged with the responsibility for a publication. The committee at first made plans for a course dealing with "general music" as a specific course in the curriculum. After the first meeting of the committee, each member was asked to consult with a working resource committee in his own geographical area to assist in defining the problem and to give the broadest possible base for the project. Further deliberations by the committee made it increasingly clear that the assignment was a much broader and more complicated one. Gradually a new concept emerged—one which made it mandatory to redefine "general music" so that it would include every phase of the music program from the concert band to the elementary classroom.

Through correspondence, additional meetings, and sessions on music in general education held in connection with various divisional and national conventions, which enabled the tentative conclusions to be shared with many Conference members, the present publication evolved. The culmination of this latter activity was at the Biennial Convention in Philadelphia in March 1964, when four general sessions were held which included demonstrations by teachers who illustrated how a general music program might be implemented through performance classes in band, orchestra, and chorus as well as through classes of a non-performing type. Members of the committee were present at all four sessions, and following each demonstration served as a panel discussion group. The demonstrations and discussions were designed to illustrate the basic concepts which the committee had described in the publication.

This publication is not to be taken as definitive in the sense that school systems will find a ready made curriculum which can be adopted in its entirety. In fact, adoption of some of the suggestions may make use of others unnecessary or even impossible. If schools are provoked into some action with respect to the role of music in general education, the committee's purposes will be served.

It is hoped that the book will prove stimulating to *all* music educators regardless of their teaching areas, and that it will function not only at the level of philosophy and objectives, but that it will influence directly the quality of the music experiences in many classrooms throughout the country in the years to come.

KARL D. ERNST

Contents

CHAPTER I

General Education
and Music

The omnipresence of music in our society—and, in fact, in most societies since the dawn of history—argues that music satisfies fundamental human needs. It is not the purpose of this book to discuss these needs or to become involved in conjectures as to just how music meets them. It is sufficient to note that the children in our schools today will be living their lives in a world in which music is more available to them than has ever been true in times past. What are the implications for the curriculum?

As the American Association of School Administrators noted in their resolution of 1959, "It is important that pupils, as a part of general education, learn to appreciate, to understand, to create, and to criticize with discrimination those products of the mind, the voice, the hand, and the body which give dignity to the person and exalt the spirit of man."[1]

General education is "common schooling," that quantity of schooling which at any particular time is normally regarded as necessary for all and made available to all. Today, the American "common" school extends from kindergarten through the twelfth grade. One function of the "common" school in the United States is to prepare young people for life in a free, democratic society in which they will have the opportunity and the responsibility to make choices. The type of choices they make in aesthetic matters will determine the culture they build for America. The schools cannot afford to send them ill-prepared into this responsible role.

---

[1] Resolution on the Creative Arts adopted by the American Association of School Administrators at the Atlantic City convention, February 18, 1959.

1

The excellent statement of the National Association of Secondary School Principals summarizes and amplifies this problem, and is equally applicable to all levels of general school experience:

> Youth today face two radically different forces. Schools push for excellence in all subjects. At the same time, the mass media outside the schools all too frequently focus students' attention on shallow, mediocre models of the good life. Students exercise value standards as they make independent, intellectual judgments about artistic quality in all of their experiences. For example, they identify the characteristics of good theatre in television or motion pictures. They discriminate among the barrage of music that permeates their world. They judge design in the goods they buy and the things they produce.
>
> All secondary-school students, therefore, need experiences in understanding music, the visual arts, the theatre arts, the industrial arts, and home economics. Otherwise they base their decisions on stereotypes and prejudices which can easily be manipulated by the mass media and by superficial shifts in fashion. Students need to learn how to exercise social responsibility in making personal and group decisions about the arts.
>
> The hulking ugliness of large parts of our cities and towns, the mediocrity of some industrial production, the brazen tawdriness of much of our advertising and commercial display, the insipid programs that fill many hours on radio and television, and the content of many pages of newspapers and magazines do not provide the desired image. These conditions exist because too many people are willing to accept such standards, having little educated basis for critical selection. In a free society, each individual is socially responsible for the quality of art he contributes in his home, his work, and his stand on the kinds of architecture and the urban and suburban planning in his community. For example, he makes many decisions about civic planning, housing, parkways, and conservation, all of which involve the arts. The arts thus viewed as a function of society are the responsibility of all citizens. . . .
>
> Neither an outstanding nation nor a worthy individual can be intellectually mature and aesthetically impoverished. School programs should reflect a balanced image of social and artistic values.[2]

Briefly, the "common" school sets preparation for the good life as an overall goal. But the good life—and the immediate school years are a part of it—requires cultural, aesthetic tastes

---

[2] National Association of Secondary-School Principals, *The Arts in the Comprehensive Secondary School.* (Washington, D.C.: The Association, 1962), pp. 4-5.

and satisfactions at an increasing level of refinement. Not only is music part of all human experience, but an important part of the good life.

In a time of great scientific and technological advances, it is important that we maintain an appropriate balance in the curriculum. Music speaks through a kind of common language which transcends some of the difficulties of the spoken word in communicating deep human feelings which are common to all men. It is able to transport us into the past, into different parts of the world, and into other seasons of the year. It can help us to understand the deep feelings of those who lived in the past, of those who speak languages not commonly understood, to play, to work, and to worship with those whose lives are lived under differing circumstances. Music and the arts must be given an increasingly important place in the curriculum of the schools for they play an increasingly important role in contemporary society.

It is granted that a hundred lifetimes would not be sufficient to explore the vast and constantly accumulating heritage of music, or to exhaust the experience to be gained from listening to or performing it. What minimum specific goals, then, does it seem reasonable to attempt to set for music in the twelve or thirteen years of the general school experience? What degree of musical maturity should *all* pupils possess as they leave the twelfth grade? What core of musical experiences should have been theirs?

CHAPTER II

Musical Outcomes

W<small>HAT</small> minimum specific goals does it seem reasonable to attempt to set for music in the twelve or thirteen years of the general school experiences? What degree of musical maturity should all pupils possess as they leave the twelfth grade? It is the purpose of this chapter to answer these two questions—to describe the desirable musical attributes of the generally educated student as he graduates from high school. *What are the outcomes expected from school music experiences?*

In describing the musical personality of the generally educated person the characteristics will be grouped under three areas. It is believed that the generally educated person will have certain minimum *skills* and *understandings* with respect to music. While he is developing these he will, at the same time, have developed *attitudes* about music; he will have included music in his system of values. In describing the attributes which can be placed under these classifications— skills, understandings, attitudes—it is inevitable that there will be some overlapping within each classification and among items from separate classifications. It is felt, however, that these eleven outcomes may help to define the task of music as a part of general education.

SKILLS

I. He will have skill in listening to music.

The generally educated person listens with a purpose. He recognizes the broad melodic and rhythmic contours of musical compositions. He is familiar with the sounds of the instruments of the orchestra and the types of human voices. He can hear and identify more than one melody at a time. He can recognize patterns of melody and rhythm when repeated in identical or in altered form. He can concentrate on sounds and the relationships between sounds.

II. He will be able to sing.

The generally educated person is articulate. He uses his voice confidently in speech and song. He sings in a way that is satisfying to himself. He can carry a part in group singing. His singing is expressive.

III. He will be able to express himself on a musical instrument.

A generally educated person is curious. He is interested in how instrumental music is produced and willing to try his hand at making music, if only at an elementary level with a percussion instrument, a recorder, or a "social-type" instrument. He experiments with providing accompaniments for singing and rhythmic activities. He is familiar with the piano keyboard.

IV. He will be able to interpret musical notation.

The generally educated person is literate. He understands arithmetical and musical symbols. He is able to respond to the musical notation of unison and simple part songs. He can follow the scores of instrumental compositions.

UNDERSTANDINGS

V. He will understand the importance of design in music.

The generally educated person understands the structure of the various disciplines. He knows the component parts of music and the interrelationships that exist between melody, rhythm, harmony, and form. He is able to recognize design elements aurally, and he uses musical notation to confirm and reinforce this recognition. He realizes that the active listener can, in a sense, share in the composer's act of creation. By understanding how music communicates, he has come to gain insight into what it communicates.

VI. He will relate music to man's historical development.

The generally educated person has historical perspective. He recognizes that music has long been an important part of man's life. He understands that its development in Western civilization is one of the unique elements of his own heritage. He is familiar with the major historical periods in that development and the styles of music which they produced. He has acquaintance with some of the musical masterpieces of the past and with the men who composed them. He relates this knowledge to his understanding of man's social and political development.

VII. He will understand the relationships existing between music and other areas of human endeavor.

The generally educated person integrates his knowledge. He has been helped to see that the arts have in common such concepts as design resulting from repetition and variation. Sociology and politics are recognized as pertinent to the development of art as well as to economics. He understands how literature and music enhance one another and together illuminate history. The mathematical and physical aspects of music are known to him through aural experiences as well as through intellectual inquiry.

VIII. He will understand the place of music in contemporary society.

The generally educated person is aware of his environment. He understands the function of music in the life of his community and he accepts some responsibility for exercising his critical judgment in order to improve the quality of music heard in church and on radio and television. He is aware of the position of the musician in today's social structure and understands the opportunities open to him to engage in musical endeavor both as a vocation and as an avocation.

ATTITUDES

IX. He will value music as a means of self-expression.

A generally educated person has developed outlets for his emotions. He recognizes music not only as a source of satisfaction because of its filling his desire for beauty, but also because of the unique way in which it expresses man's feelings. If he is not prepared to gain release by actually performing music, he has learned to experience this vicariously. He looks to music as a source of renewal of mind and body, as an evidence of beneficence in his life. He recognizes the importance of performers and composers and is grateful for the pleasure and inspiration which they give him.

X. He will desire to continue his musical experiences.

The generally educated person continues to grow. He seeks additional experiences in areas in which he has found satisfaction. He looks for community musical activities in which he can participate. He attends concerts and listens to music on radio, television, and recordings. He keeps informed concerning happenings in the world of music by reading newspapers and magazines.

XI. He will discriminate with respect to music.

The generally educated person has good taste. He has learned to make sensitive choices based upon musical knowledge and skill in listening. He evaluates performances and exercises mature judgments in this area. He is not naive with respect to the functional use of music for commercial purposes nor to the commercial pressures which will be exerted to obtain what money he can spend for music.

The realization of these outcomes presents a challenge of considerable magnitude to the music educators of America. As a set of even minimum goals they may appear remote from the current situation in many communities today. Remoteness of an objective is not an unfamiliar situation for the profession, however. Consider the progress made towards the establishment of a truly musical nation since the days of music education in a frontier society. Let us assure ourselves that nothing less than these outcomes, or a comparable set of objectives, is acceptable as a goal for music in general education.

CHAPTER III

Organizing
Music Experiences

Musical learnings are the responsibility of the whole school. They cannot be assigned to one teacher and forgotten by the others. Education in music begins in the pre-school years and continues until the student graduates from high school; it does not come about as the result of a course in the junior high school years. It is, rather, the product of everything musical that happens in twelve or thirteen years of schooling, indeed of everything musical that happens throughout a lifetime.

All of the teachers and the principal need to be concerned about education in music—for the English teacher may make a very real contribution to one or more of the outcomes mentioned in Chapter II; or the principal, by his demonstrated interest in music or by the assembly programs he schedules, may set an example of a mature person's relationship with music. Even though this total involvement of the school exists, all of the outcomes will not be realized unless some teachers have special concern in seeing that they are achieved. It is the music teachers—all of them, band and choir directors, class piano teachers, string specialists, teachers of music history, music consultants—to whom this task rightly falls.

CURRICULUM PLANNING

There are many ways of organizing the curriculum to realize the outcomes. Curriculum planning should involve many persons and not be left to individual teachers. It is not impossible to achieve the desired outcomes through requiring all students to take a common course but this is by no means the only, or even the most desirable, approach. A single required course has probably been the most used method and, as a result, is apt to be the plan which will bring the least amount of new thought to the problem. It will be the path of least resistance for many schools but it is likely to result in only a token attempt at a program of general education in music. Yet, with a strong teacher, it is conceivable that such a course may serve some school systems very well.

Music educators must accept this challenge of becoming effective teachers. The profession must provide the schools with teachers who are both able and eager to lead all students to the desired outcomes. Many of the suggestions to be found in Chapter IV, "The Nature of the Experiences," can be used within the framework of existing courses by teachers who will seek their satisfactions in areas other than conducting public performances. It is hoped also that the ideas in Chapter IV may serve to stimulate the imaginations of teachers in order that the content of all the music offerings may be strengthened. All schools, however, are encouraged to reexamine their total music curriculum rather than merely to appliqué some new experiences on the established structure.

One of the problems often faced by curriculum developers in the junior high school has been to decide whether students in performing groups should be excused from required music classes. This has been a problem because the goals of the classes and the goals of the performing groups were not seen to be the same. If the outcomes of Chapter II are accepted as the goals for both types of experience, the problem evaporates. The performing groups then have the potential for becoming one of the ways of achieving the common goals not only for those students in the ensembles but for the school as a whole. The music they play and sing is selected for its value in educating for general education goals, as well as for the development of performance skills. The performances that the groups work toward are educational concerts for the other students. The choir, the band, the orchestra, the small ensembles become laboratory groups to help all pupils in the school achieve the goals of general education. Students in music classes contribute to the education of the performers in turn, through the preparation of background material, program notes, bulletin board displays, and articles for school publications.

Some schools might organize such a program around a music class that included all pupils on some days and split into rehearsal sections, listening sections, library sections, and laboratory sections on other days. Another school may find it more successful to concentrate the efforts of the music teacher on the performing groups and the preparation of a regular series of assembly programs that would be structured to meet general education outcomes. A third plan might call for all students to take a brief course of orientation in music and then allow the pupils to initiate projects of their own to develop a program that would help them achieve all eleven outcomes. In such a plan, the music teacher becomes a counselor and advisor.

Instrumental Music.—Some school systems have developed extensive programs of instrumental music that involve a large percentage of the student body. Such a program is defensible but it must be remembered that the objectives for instrumental music do not supersede, or exist apart from, the aims of a general education in music. Participation in instrumental music represents an area of specialized activity through which the development and application of the technical skills of performance enhance the opportunities for the individual's association with, and involvement in, music. The premise that instrumental music has for its major objective the development of technical, manipulative and reading skills falls short of realizing the objectives of music education.

A perspective of the possible contribution of the school band (for example) to the aims of education in music is provided in the following statements:

The school band is a part of a general program in music education, and this fact, I feel, should not be forgotten. It is not enough to train or drill youngsters to play notes on an instrument. This is a mechanical acquisition, although a valuable one, and represents specialized training rather than general education. The band can be an extremely valuable adjunct to general education, provided the participants receive some idea of what their skills are meant to serve, and acquire some familiarity with the art of music itself.[1]

How, then, will instrumental music relate to general education in music? Participation in secondary school bands and orchestras *extends* rather than replaces the content and experiences that are the substance of music classes. The school instrumental organizations become, in part, a laboratory in which the structure, design, and meaning of music can be demonstrated and made more functional through the added factor of involvement and participation on a skilled level. If instrumental music is to supplement the general education program in producing musically knowledgeable, discriminating, culturally-aware, musically literate persons, instrumental music will *develop concepts*, will have *structured content*, and will *align its practices* so that the larger aims of music education can be realized.

Vocal Music.—Just as a properly planned curriculum in instrumental music can realize the desired outcomes, so also can a vocal music program be designed to serve both general and special education. Choral organizations and small ensembles can be used to develop musical understandings at the same time that they provide practical experience leading to the development of vocal skills.

Integrated Learnings.—The unified humanities course is finding increasing favor at the senior high school level. A great many of the eleven outcomes can be pursued directly in such an organizational scheme. Performing students are a part of the instructional force in the best of these. Special arrangements may be necessary to assure the acquisition of certain skills by all the students. Programmed learning is

---

[1] Richard Franko Goldman, *The Wind Band.* (Boston: Allyn and Bacon, Inc., 1961), pp. 253-54. © Reprinted by permission of McIntosh and Otis, Inc.

a new technique with promise in the area of notation and elementary theory.[2] Team teaching has much to recommend it for integrated courses. A situation to be avoided is one in which teachers are asked to teach what they do not really know.

It should be mentioned that certain of the musical outcomes are more easily realized with older students. Some of the interrelationships with other subjects lend themselves better to the history and literature studied in high school than to the material of the junior high school years. Because of this it is thought inadvisable for schools to attempt to realize the major portion of the goals by the end of the ninth grade. It has been argued in the past that the schedule of the senior high school did not permit a course in music for all students and that if such a course were to be required, it would have to be in the junior high school. This was at one time more of a problem than it is now, as change is being felt in the organizational design of the secondary school curriculum. Ideas such as team teaching, modules of time, and programmed learning are beginning to have effect on the rigidity of school schedules. As new patterns emerge, the musical outcomes described in Chapter II must be kept before those who organize the curriculum in order that provision is made for realizing these broader objectives.

EVALUATION

Any educational program worth planning and executing needs to be evaluated to determine how successful it is. This evaluation can be of two types—an evaluation of the degree to which individual students are attaining the outcomes, and an evaluation of the change in behavior of the graduates of the program as a whole. There are things to be said in favor of each type. The first is easier to administer and may provide motivation for the students to strive to realize the goals. Successful completion of a comprehensive examination in

[2] See for example John Clough, *Scales, Intervals, Keys and Trials.* (New York: W. W. Norton & Company, Inc., 1964.)

music as a prerequisite for graduation might insure respect for instruction in music.

The second type of evaluation would give a truer measure of the success of the program though it does not contain the motivational feature. Since the outcomes sought by the program are desired to be lifelong, rather than those that are attained merely for the purpose of passing a test, it must be admitted that this type of evaluation is needed.

There are several implications inherent in the use of this second type of evaluation. The curriculum must be very carefully structured to assure that all eleven outcomes are being taught for, since the burden of proof is on the school and the education it is providing, rather than on the student who must jump a hurdle in order to graduate. Motivation of the students must be intrinsic rather than extrinsic. Evaluation of the program of general education in music will involve follow-up studies of the graduates and periodic analysis of the musical life of the community.

CONCLUSION

This brief discussion of organizational problems indicates the necessity for rethinking the place of music in the school day. Rigidity of schedules and inflexibility of physical facilities may, in the past, have prevented music educators from achieving what they hoped to accomplish. Many times, however, administrators made no vigorous attempt to accommodate new programs in music because these programs were not sufficiently prepared or adequately defended. The time will never be better than the present for changing the situation. Change[3] is now a part of the school scene and one group of administrators has recently set down the general goals for music[4] in the comprehensive secondary school. It is believed that if music educators present their administrators with well-conceived objectives and a plan for achieving them, the assistance they need in organizing the experiences will be forthcoming.

[3] J. Lloyd Trump and Dorsey Baynham. *Focus on Change*. (Chicago: Rand McNally & Company, 1961.)

[4] National Association of Secondary School Principals, *op. cit.*, pp. 8-9.

CHAPTER IV

The Nature
of the Experiences

CHAPTER I of this book closed with three questions. Two of these have been dealt with in the discussion of musical outcomes. The third, "What core of musical experiences should have been provided all high school graduates?", remains unanswered. It is the purpose of this chapter to indicate the nature of the experiences that might lead to the desired outcomes.

THE CONTENT OF EDUCATION IN MUSIC

The content of music education as a part of general education can be as broad as the field of music itself. The descriptions of experiences here will be in fairly general terms as it is not the purpose of this book to set down a curriculum that might be adopted by a school system. On the other hand, some very specific examples of materials are given. It is hoped that this approach may serve to fire the imagination of music teachers in all areas of the curriculum in order that they may devise better means of making their contribution to the development of broadly educated persons.

Content Areas.—A subject as large and complex as music demands division into smaller units in order that it may be discussed intelligently. It must be admitted, however, that any such division will be arbitrary and that much overlapping will be inevitable. For the convenience of discussion of desirable music experiences, eleven content areas have been selected. All of these relate directly to the outcomes of Chapter II, but the relationship is not a one to one relationship and the presence of eleven items in each of the lists is pure coincidence.

The eleven selected content areas to be used are as follows:

1. Elements of Music
2. Form and Design in Music
3. Interpretive Aspects of Music
4. Science of Sound
5. The Musical Score
6. Historical Considerations
7. Music and Man
8. Music as a Form of Expression
9. Types of Musical Performance
10. Relationship of Music to Other Disciplines in the Humanities
11. Music Today

Together these eleven areas constitute one route which *could* lead to the desired outcomes. No implication that this is the only route is intended. Each school system will need to devise its own plan for reaching outcomes such as those described in Chapter II.

Readers are urged not to consider suggestions in the content areas merely as outlines for units in a music course though some may be useful for this purpose. Rather, these are experiences with potential for leading to the outcomes of Chapter II. The experiences may be provided in many different ways over a period of several years and need to be incorporated in a school-wide curriculum of music for general education.

The format which will be used in describing these content areas deals with four aspects of the music program.

1. *Experiences All Music Classes Should Provide.* In each of the content areas these basic experiences will be for all students in the school regardless of the particular classes they take.

2. *Special Experiences for Nonselective Music Classes.* These experiences are especially appropriate for students enrolled in a music class which does not have musical performance as one of its major goals.

3. *Special Experiences for Instrumental Music Classes.* These experiences are especially appropriate in instrumental classes and ensemble rehearsals.

4. *Special Experiences for Vocal Music Classes.* These experiences are especially appropriate in vocal classes and choral rehearsals.

In addition to the special experiences in each of the last three categories, all music classes should provide the experiences listed in category number one.

Content Area 1

ELEMENTS OF MUSIC

A. Rhythm

Experiences All Music Classes Should Provide

In order that all students may understand the primary importance of rhythm in music they should be provided with opportunities to:

1. Experience the underlying pulsations in music. A comparison of the rhythmic similarities found in the Baroque Concertos of Vivaldi and Bach with some Dixieland jazz may be helpful.

2. Demonstrate that they understand the relationship between duration and pulse.

3. Determine the basic metric pattern of music they hear, and understand that most music when reduced to its basic meter will move in twos or threes. The application of this to social dancing should be noted. Analysis of compound meters, irregular meters, and multimeters with the resultant effects on the character of the music should also be undertaken.

4. Observe the expressive use of accents in music.

5. Experiment with periods of sound and silence to create satisfying patterns. Such experiences should involve sound-producing instruments which can sustain tone as well as the more limited percussion instruments in order that an understanding of the importance of duration to rhythm may be properly established.

6. Develop awareness of rhythm in nature and in many artistic expressions of man.

7. Observe the importance of the rhythmic principles of recurrence or alternation in the organizational structure of musical forms. Students should analyze such forms of music as the rounded binary, ternary, sonata-allegro, and rondo. They should be made conscious of the rhythmic effect created by the various entries in a fugue or a motet.

8. Understand rhythm through bodily movement. This should include experiences that will help students recognize the contribution rhythm makes to such characteristic dances as the polka, schottische, jig, minuet, waltz, hornpipe, reel, and march. Bodily movement might also be employed to help students understand the rhythmic (architectonic) nature of musical forms.

9. Develop an awareness to and an understanding of the properties of rhythm as used in contemporary music—changing meter, polyrhythms, syncopation, irregular accents. Such experiences might involve dividing the class into groups to perform different metric patterns simultaneously, clapping a syncopated rhythm against the sound of a metronome, listening to two metric patterns simultaneously on such a device as the Trinome.

10. Experience ways in which composers increase rhythmic interest through variations such as changing durational patterns in augmentation and diminution.

11. Have experiences which will increase their ability to think rhythmically. Canonic rhythmic imitation between the teacher and class might be one such exercise. (Teacher claps a rhythmic pattern and student follows one measure

later repeating the pattern he has just heard but at the same time listening for the next measure he is to imitate.) Simple Dalcroze exercises are valuable for all.

Special Experiences for Nonselective Music Classes

In music classes where performance is not a major objective, students can develop an increased understanding of rhythm if they are motivated to:

1. Use graphic notation (long and short dashes) to represent the melodic rhythms of songs and recorded music.

2. Clap or tap rhythmic patterns or play them on percussion instruments.

3. Study the means by which the system of staff notation indicates rhythmic characteristics of music. How is duration indicated? Accent? Change in tempo? (See also Content Area 4.)

4. Chant the melodic rhythms of songs and poems.

5. Learn to conduct the class as it sings and plays.

6. Analyze music to identify its rhythmic characteristics including patterns of rhythm that are repeated.

7. Characterize and discuss the rhythmic qualities of composers, periods, and forms of music being studied.

8. Create and notate instrumentations for percussion ensembles. Students might prepare for this by converting a rhythmic four-part song they are singing into notation for percussion instruments.

9. Use varied types of bodily movement to develop recognition of the rhythmic characteristics of music being studied, particularly dance forms.

Special Experiences for Instrumental and Vocal Music Classes

Since to understand a piece of music thoroughly it is necessary to know its rhythmic structure, all school performing groups as part of their regular course of study should:

1. Conduct, clap, and chant rhythmic patterns in compositions being studied as a means to aid precise performance.

2. Use French time names or other such counting devices to demonstrate an understanding of meter and phrase rhythms.

3. Analyze the music being studied, recognizing the rhythmic characteristics which give the composition its distinctive quality or mood.

4. Relate the rhythmic characteristics of a composition to the period, style, and idiom which it represents. Students will want to listen to recorded performances of the composition or of representative compositions to gain perspective on the use of rhythm in musical communication.

5. Discover the principal rhythmic motives which are used repeatedly in selections being rehearsed. These motives might be analyzed to attempt to determine why each is effective.

6. Discover during rehearsal of a composition the parts to be played or sung which serve what is primarily a rhythmic function.

7. Give careful attention to rhythmic subleties in the music being studied, making certain that they are properly executed (e.g., ♩♩♩ is not ♫♩ and ♩ ♪ is not ♩♫).

The following brief list contains suggestions of works of particular rhythmic interest which might be used with school groups.

ORCHESTRA

Easy

| Bartók | Five Pieces for Younger Orchestras | Remick |
| Mussorgsky | Cossack Dance | C. Fischer |

Medium

| Bergsma | Paul Bunyan Suite | C. Fischer |
| Dvořák | Slavonic Dance No. 1 | Berlin |

Difficult

Beethoven	Egmont Overture	C. Fischer
Copland	An Outdoor Overture	Boosey & Hawkes
Riegger	Dance Rhythms	Associated

STRING ORCHESTRA

Medium

Trew	Miniature Quartet	Novello

Difficult

Debussy	Quartet No. 10—Scherzo	Elkan-Vogel, Kalmus
Piston	String Quartet No. 2	G. Schirmer

BAND

Easy

Handel-Ford	Baroque Suite	Pro Art

Medium

Holst	Hammersmith	Boosey & Hawkes
Kechley	Suite for Band	Associated
Persichetti	Pageant	C. Fischer

Difficult

Jacob	Flag of Stars	Boosey & Hawkes
Lecuona	Malaguena	Marks
Mennin	Canzona	C. Fischer
Wagner-Cailliet	Invocation of Albrecht	Fox

CHORAL-SATB

Easy

Glarum	Sing Praises	SHM
Morley	Now Is the Month of Maying	Gray

Medium

Bright	Lament of the Enchantress	Associated
Handel	Hallelujah, Amen	Gray
Persichetti	Jimmie's Got a Goil	G. Schirmer

Difficult

Berger	Brazilian Psalm	G. Schirmer
Lubin	Marching Song	Boston

CHORAL-SA and SSA

Easy

Cowan, arr.	Waltzing Matilda	C. Fischer
Loesser-Simeone	Thumbelina	Shawnee

Medium

Arcadelt	Ave Maria	Bourne
Bartók	Wooing of a Girl	Boosey & Hawkes

Difficult

Durante	Danza, Danza, Fanciulla Gentile	Lawson-Gould

FILMS

African Rhythms	Association
Bolero	Avis
Elements of Composition	Indiana
Indian Dances	Encyclopaedia Britt.
Meter and Rhythm	NET
Modern Music	NET
Pacific 231	McGraw-Hill
Rhythm	NET
Rhythm and Percussion	EBF
Rhythm in Music	Coronet
Rhythm Instruments and Movements	EBF
Rhythm Is Everywhere	Mahnke
Rhythm of the Drum	UMTV

FILMSTRIPS

Rhythm Magic Series (3 films)	McGraw-Hill

BIBLIOGRAPHY

Brown, Calvin S. *Music and Literature; A Comparison of the Arts.*

Cooper, Grosvenor, and Leonard B. Meyer. *The Rhythmic Structure of Music.*

Gardner, Helen. *Art Through the Ages.*

Goldstein, Harriet, and Vetta Goldstein. *Art in Everyday Life.*

Ronga, Lugi. *The Meeting of Poetry and Music.*

Sachs, Curt. *The Commonwealth of Art.*

Sachs, Curt. *Rhythm and Tempo.*

Toch, Ernst. *The Shaping Forces of Music.*

Wold, Milo A., and Edmund Cyker. *Introduction to Music and Art in the Western World.*

(Detailed bibliographical information on these items will be found in bibliography at the end of the book.)

B. MELODY

Experiences All Music Classes Should Provide

Melody, as the most obvious of the elements of music, may be understood only superficially unless there is conscious effort to grasp its relationships to rhythm, harmony, and form as well as the subtleties of the phenomenon of melody itself. All students, therefore, should be provided with opportunities to:

1. Develop an understanding of melody as a succession of musical tones ordered in time. They should experience, through singing and/or playing, melodies that are smooth and graceful as well as those that are sharply angular.

2. Experiment with tonal movement—up, down, or repetition—and tonal organization—step, half step, skip, or leap. After students have developed the skill to differentiate aurally between these types of movement, the visual representation of the movements should be introduced. (See Content Area 4.)

3. Develop an understanding of tonal groupings such as the motive, phrase, sequence, and theme.

4. Observe the ways in which range, register, and length of melodic grouping contribute to melodic meaning.

5. Develop an understanding of the ways rhythm organizes tones in a melody to give it a distinctive musical meaning. The practice of identifying melodies from their rhythmic patterns might help demonstrate this, as could the altering of the rhythmic structure of well-known tunes. The importance of the rhythm of words in song should be stressed and the free rhythm of Gregorian chant contrasted with the setting of a poem with a regular meter.

6. Sense and to understand the tension and release of active and rest tones and the ways they are organized into the scales and modes of the Western system of tonality. This would include experience with major, minor, chromatic, and whole tone scales.

7. Use intervallic relationships as the precise means of measuring distances between the tones of a melody.

8. Develop an understanding of the importance of melody in the music of other cultures. This might include also the concept of racial or national melodic characteristics such as the use of the pentatonic scale by the American Indian or the Scotch, the florid nature of the music of the Middle East, or the angular nature of the Swiss yodel.

9. Gain a perspective on the relationship of melody to the various periods and styles of Western music—Renaissance, Baroque, Classic, Romantic, Impressionistic, Expressionistic. This would include opportunity to experience melody in both homophonic and polyphonic textures. (Also see Content Area 6—Historical Considerations.)

10. Become aware of the constant search and experimentation by composers to find new ways to organize melody. This might involve contact with a composer who works with the twelve tone row or with electronic music.

11. Develop a sensitivity to melodic elements in their environment and an understanding of how composers have used such sounds realistically and stylistically (e.g., Beethoven's *Pastoral Symphony* or Gershwin's *An American in Paris*).

12. Expand their understanding of the relationship between melody and harmony to enable them to comprehend the statement by Ernst Toch that "Melodies, by combination, integrate into harmony; . . . harmony, by dissolution, disintegrates into melody. The two phenomena, melody and harmony, are linked, not closely, but inextricably together."[1]

13. Discover the role that melody plays in the various forms of music (e.g., sing songs such as "Au Clair de la Lune" or "Drink to Me Only With Thine Eyes" to determine how melodic repetition helps organize the music into a pattern—AABA). Do the same with a more extended song such as Purcell's "I Attempt from Love's Sickness To Fly" to understand rondo form. Assign the themes of the first

[1] Ernst Toch, *The Shaping Forces of Music*. (New York: Criterion Music Corp., 1948), p. 64. Permission granted by Criterion Music Corp.

movement of Mozart's *Eine Kleine Nachtmusik* to sections of the class who raise their hands when "their melody" appears. Study how Wagner uses the melodic fragments (leitmotiv) "Grief," "Isolde's Magic," "Tristan," "Look," "Love Potion," "Death," "Magic Casket," and "Deliverance by Death," to construct the Prelude to the first act of *Tristan and Isolde*. (See Ernest Newman's *Stories of the Great Operas*.)

Special Experiences for Nonselective Music Classes

In music classes where performance is not a major objective, the students may be assisted in developing an understanding of melody if they:

1. Diagram the movement of melody with hand movements while listening or while singing.

2. Devise graphic means of representing the contour of a melody on paper or on the chalk board.

3. Search for examples of melody that demonstrate such characteristic patterns as use of a scale, outlining a chord, or repeated notes.

4. Write scale and modal patterns and play them on melody instruments.

5. Create melodies utilizing various scale patterns and learn to notate them.

6. Compare the melodic characteristics of musical styles and periods.

7. Learn to recognize intervals aurally and visually and to utilize this skill in singing and playing.

8. Use the musical score to observe the ways composers achieve melodic interest through such devices as changing modes, shifting registers, transposition, embellishments, and timbre.

Special Experiences for Instrumental and Vocal Classes

An understanding of melody can be developed in performing groups if the students are encouraged to:

1. Analyze the melodies of the compositions being studied and to relate them to the appropriate scales and modes. Special attention should be given to the problems of performance associated with any of these scale patterns.

2. Demonstrate individually that they understand the importance to melodic expression of such concepts as the rise and fall of a phrase, active and rest tones, or the necessity for varying the interpretation of a repeated melodic pattern.

3. Experiment with varied tempi and dynamic levels to determine the most effective interpretation of a melody. (See Content Area 3—Interpretive Aspects of Music.)

4. Gain an understanding of how melody is used in various periods, styles, and by composers. If this does not develop to a sufficiently comprehensive degree from the music performed in class, students should be assisted in carrying out a program of listening to live and recorded music that will complement their performing experiences.

5. Analyze the musical score while instruments or voices perform only the main structural melodies of the composition, i.e., without accompaniment or counter melodies. This might be followed by a reversal of the procedure. (The choruses of Mendelssohn provide good opportunity for this; e.g., "How Lovely Are the Messengers," or "He, Watching Over Israel.")

Suggestions for materials that might be used to teach some of these melodic concepts follow.

ORCHESTRA

Easy

MacDowell-Isaac	To a Wild Rose	C. Fischer
Purcell	Trumpet Tune and Air	Boosey & Hawkes
Gluck-Mottl	Petit Suite de Ballet	C. Fischer

Medium

Cimarosa	Overture to The Secret Marriage	Boosey & Hawkes
Mozart-Beeler	Alleluia, *Exultate Jubilate*	G. Schirmer
Schubert-Weaver	*Rosamunde* Overture	Mills

Difficult

Bruch	Kol Nidrei	G. Schirmer
Saint-Saëns	Bacchanale	C. Fischer

ENSEMBLES

Easy

Beethoven-Urban	Minuet in G (String Quartet)	Mills
Handel-Bauer	Six Little Fugues (Woodwind Quintet)	Boston
Haydn	Menuetto—Quartet No. 52 (String Quartet)	Presser

Medium

Bach	Fugues 1, 2, & 3 (Brass Quartet)	Mills
Johnson	Cremona String Quartet Folio	C. Fischer

Difficult

DesPres	Royal Fanfare (Brass Quartet)	R. King
Luening	Fuguing Tune (Woodwind Quintet)	Associated
Mason	Variations on a Tune by Powell (String Quartet)	Oxford
Stevens	Theme and Variations (String Quartet)	Mills

BAND

Easy

Ortone, arr.	Londonderry Air	Pro Art
Handel-Gordon	Air and Finale from the *Water Music*	Fox
Prokofiev-Lang	Gavotte from *Classical Symphony*	Mills

Medium

Bach-Leidzen	Jesu, Joy of Man's Desiring	C. Fischer
Debussy-Johnson	Reverie	Rubank
Wagner-Osterling	*Die Meistersinger*, excerpts	Ludwig

Difficult

Bernstein	*West Side Story* Selection	G. Schirmer
Boyer-Lillya	Ariana Overture	Witmark
Milhaud	Suite Française	Leeds

CHORAL-SATB

Easy

Ehret, arr.	Great Day	Lawson-Gould
Gilmore	When Johnny Comes Marching Home	Summy-Birchard
Holst	Turn Back O Man	Galaxy

Medium

Bach	O Rejoice, Ye Christians, Loudly	E. C. Schirmer
Mendelssohn	He, Watching Over Israel	G. Schirmer
Zingarelli	Go Not Far From Me, O God	Gray

Difficult

Brahms	How Lovely Is Thy Dwelling Place	G. Schirmer
Hindemith	Six Chansons	Associated
Wilbye	Come Shepherd Swains	Associated

CHORAL-SA

Easy

Schubert-Coleman	To Music	Oxford

Medium

Erb, arr.	TuTu Maramba	Lawson-Gould
Roberton	Westering Home	Oxford

FILMS

Alphabet in Black	NET
Alphabet in White	NET
Ancient Chinese Music	Harmon
The Earth Sings (Israel)	Brandon
Elements of Composition	NET
Indian Dances	EBF
Key Feeling	NET
Major and Minor Tonalities	NET
Melody in Music	Coronet
Melody of Hindustan	IFB
Modern Music	NET
The Musical Phrase	NET
Musical Words	NET
Rondo Form	NET
The Sonata	NET
Song Form	NET

BIBLIOGRAPHY

Finn, William J. "The Conductor as a Re-Creator," "The Locale of Melody," and "Modality" from *The Art of the Choral Conductor,* Volume II.

Newman, Ernest. *Stories of the Great Operas.*

Rubsamen, Walter H. "Melody," *The International Cyclopedia of Music and Musicians.* Ninth edition.

Scholes, Percy A. "Melody." *The Oxford Companion to Music.*

(Detailed bibliographical information on these items will be found in the bibliography at the end of the book.)

C. HARMONY

Experiences All Music Classes Should Provide

Harmony is that element which is most unique to the music of the Western world. To properly understand the music of their culture, students must develop an appreciation of the role of harmony. To this end all students should have opportunities to:

1. Produce harmony.

2. Advance their understanding of the expressive qualities of consonance and dissonance.

3. Learn how chords are organized and the manner in which they are related to tonal centers.

4. Expand their knowledge of the use of chords in homophonic texture and of their relationship to melody. (See No. 12, p. 24.)

5. Develop an understanding of the role of chords in establishing cadences and in modulation.

6. Study forms of music which are predominantly homophonic in texture.

7. Experience the ways in which polyphonic music is organized. These should involve such devices as imitation, canon, augmentation, diminution, inversion, retrograde, stretto, ostinato, and pedal point.

8. Study forms of music which are predominantly polyphonic in texture.

9. Be exposed to contemporary harmonic practices including 9th, 11th, and 13th chords, polytonality, tone clusters, and chords using intervals of the 4th and 5th.

10. Develop an historical perspective of harmonic development.

11. Study musical scores which will relate visual symbols to harmonic characteristics studied. (See Content Area 5— The Musical Score.)

Special Experiences for Nonselective Music Classes

In the music classes not designed primarily for the performance of music, students can gain a better understanding of harmony if they are encouraged to:

1. Play harmonic instruments—autoharp, guitar, piano, harmonica, ukulele, and organ.

2. Chord vocally to sense harmonies inherent in melody.

3. Write out (in order to play and sing) the chord structures of the tonic, dominant, dominant seventh, and subdominant in frequently used major and minor keys.

4. Analyze songs and instrumental themes to determine harmonies that can be used to develop accompaniments. When several possibilities exist, students should experiment to determine which is most effective.

5. Experiment with vocal and piano chording in order to understand the need for chord inversions. (e.g., Demonstrate the ease with which one can play the progression from the tonic chord in root position to the dominant seventh in first inversion (omitting the 5th) on the piano. Sing it in three parts and then chord vocally while someone sings *Skip to My Lou* or *Blow the Man Down*.

6. Experiment with examples of consonance and dissonance in order to become aware of their expressive qualities in serious music being studied. (The classic example of *Chopsticks* might be the starting point but should lead to the Chopin *Prelude*, Op. 28, No. 4, or the *Ballade*, Op. 38, or such a simple beginner's piece as David Kraehenbuehl's *Sleeping Beauty*.)

7. Create dissonant music on the piano.

8. Listen to music of contemporary composers to become aurally aware of the ways in which they use harmony.

9. Experiment with the production of organum, parallel movement, and polytonality using a familiar song such as *America*.

10. Improvise harmony; try barbershopping; sing in 3rds or 6ths; sing the chord roots. (Try *Dear Evalina* or *Stars of*

the Summer Night for barber shopping; Woody Guthrie's *So Long* or Bortniansky's *Vesper Song* for singing in 3rds and 6ths or for chording.)

11. Sing and play descants, canons, and ostinato patterns. Evaluate the verticle relationships they produce.

Special Experiences for Instrumental and Vocal Music Classes

In those classes in which music is studied by performing it, students should be given ample opportunity to study the harmonic structure of the music. They may gain a better comprehension of the role of harmony if they:

1. Analyze the music being performed, writing out the principal chords employed as well as their inversions.

2. Make a list of chord progressions frequently encountered in the music being performed and learn to recognize these when heard.

3. Learn to recognize the roles played by certain notes of chords in the creation of tension and release and develop the habit of performing these notes expressively.

4. Learn to relate one's own part to the total harmonic scheme by listening to it in relation to other parts.

5. Learn to recognize distinguishing harmonic characteristics of periods of music history, styles of musical composition, and of individual composers as represented in the music being studied.

The following list contains a few examples of typical performance material for school groups which might be used to enhance students' understanding of the role of harmony.

ORCHESTRA

Easy

| Bach-Marcelli | Choral-Fugue "All Glory" | C. Fischer |
| Elgar-Akers | Pomp and Circumstance | C. Fischer |

Medium

Brahms-Leinsdorf	O God Thou Holiest	Broude
Corelli-Muller	Adagio and Allegro	Ludwig
Debussy-Gordon	Clair de Lune	Elkan-Vogel

Difficult

Hovhaness	Prelude and Quadruple Fugue	Associated
Mussorgsky-Reibold	The Great Gate of Kiev	FitzSimons
Tchaikovsky	Symphony No. 6	Kalmus

STRING QUARTET

Medium

Debussy	Quartet No. 10	Elkan-Vogel, Kalmus
Gabrieli	Three Ricercari	Presser

BAND

Easy

Carter	Polyphonic Suite	Ludwig
Morrissey	Cathedral Echoes	Hansen
Sibelius-Goldman	Onward, Ye Peoples	Galaxy

Medium

Bach-Cailliet	Chorale and Fugue	Henri Elkan
Brown-Akers	On the Esplanade	C. Fischer
Strauss-Davis	Zueignung	Ludwig

Difficult

Beethoven	Egmont Overture	Boosey & Hawkes
Hanson	Chorale and Alleluia	C. Fischer
Schuman	Chester	Presser

CHORAL-SATB

Easy

Chajes	Song of Galilee	Transcontinental
Palestrina	Gloria Patri	Kjos
Williams	Let There Be Music	Flammer

Medium

Alcock	Voix Celestes	Chappell
Banchieri	Counterpoint of the Animals	Bourne
Williams	Roots and Leaves	SHM

Difficult

Beadell	A Prayer to the Night	Summy-Birchard
Thompson	Alleluia	E. C. Schirmer
Vittoria	O Vos Omnes	G. Schirmer

CHORAL-SA and SSA

Easy

Bach-Titcomb	Now Let All the Earth Adore Thee	Wood
Farrant-Stone	Call to Remembrance	Pro Art

Medium

Clokey   Blue Are Her Eyes   Summy-Birchard

Difficult

Holst   Now Sleeps The Crimson   Gray
                       Petal

FILMS

Afternoon of a Faun   Brandon
Appalachian Spring   Rembrandt
Harmony in Music   Coronet
Modern Music   NET
Music and Emotion   NET
The Musical Phrase   NET
Personality in Music   NET

D. TIMBRE

Experiences All Music Classes Should Provide

It is the duty of all music teachers to make their pupils aware of the broad range of tone color found in music. The general experiences of all students should therefore include the opportunity to:

1. Develop the ability to recognize the various tone colors of instruments through hearing them played by fellow students, teachers, adults in the community, on recordings, or in films.

2. Study the historical development of instruments. (e.g., Students should have some idea of the evolution of valved brass instruments from the natural horn, the development of the piano from the harpsichord and clavichord, or the evolution of the bow for stringed instruments. Such study should include relating these developments to the music that was made possible by these improvements.)

3. Develop an understanding of the nature of sound, the physical laws affecting the rate of vibration, and how such information applies to each family of instruments.

4. Study the phenomenon of vibrato as it relates to tone quality.

5. Develop an understanding of the overtone series and how it relates to the timbre of different instruments.

6. Gain some familiarity with interesting ways in which composers have used instruments in their compositions. (e.g., A study of the tone poem as a form of descriptive music that makes great use of tonal color might involve Strauss' *Till Eulenspiegel*, Smetana's *Moldau,* or Dukas' *The Sorcerer's Apprentice.*)

7. Relate human voices to families of instruments in order to understand that each family has soprano, alto, tenor, and bass members.

8. Experiment with classifying human voices as soprano, alto, tenor, or bass by their quality.

Special Experiences for Nonselective Music Classes

In those classes in which performance of music is not a major objective, students should have the opportunity to:

1. Produce musical sounds on stringed instruments, brasses, reeds, flute, piano, bells, and percussion instruments.

2. Play instruments in class where this is feasible. Such experiences might include improvising accompaniments for singing using the recorder, the open strings of the string bass or cello, resonator bells, the piano, and various kinds of drums and percussion instruments.

3. Become familiar with the instrumentation of various instrumental groups—the orchestra, the band, various chamber ensembles.

4. Follow an orchestral score while listening to a performance.

5. Make field trips to hear electronic and pipe organs.

6. Hear school, community, and professional instrumental and vocal groups in rehearsal and in concert.

7. Read poetry, such as that of Vachel Lindsey, Carl Sandburg, or Gertrude Stein, which emphasizes color of the sounds of words.

Special Experiences for Instrumental Music Classes

School instrumental groups have the opportunity to gain first-hand experience with tonal color. They should also serve other students in the school and in elementary schools by giving demonstration performances. A better understanding of tone color might be gained through regular rehearsals if the students:

1. Make special note of unique parts of compositions which have been scored in a particularly appropriate way for certain instruments.

2. Trade parts to illustrate how some melodic styles are more suitable for one instrument than for another.

3. Listen to recordings of the original version of a composition that has been transcribed for the performing group (e.g., a Bach *Prelude and Fugue* for organ that has been transcribed for band or orchestra).

4. Demonstrate for other members of the group how tones on an instrument may be altered through mutes, bowing styles, pizzicato, ways of tonguing, etc.

5. Discuss and utilize the singing approach to the production of tone on instruments.

6. Develop a song approach to phrasing.

7. Become familiar with the text and original setting of art songs, folk songs, and choral works which have been adapted for an instrumental group.

Suggestions for materials which might be used with instrumental groups in making students more aware of timbre follow.

ORCHESTRA

Easy

Handel-Anderson	Song of Jupiter (Where'er You Walk)	Mills
Luther-McLin	A Mighty Fortress	Pro Art
Saint-Saëns	Praise Ye The Lord of Hosts	Pro Art
Walter, arr.	Londonderry Air	Berkeley

Medium

Bach-Cailliet	Sheep May Safely Graze	Boosey & Hawkes
Bach-Herfurth	Arioso from "Cantata No. 156"	C. Fischer
Bach-Tolmage	Now Let Every Tongue Adore	Staff

Bizet-Seredy	*Carmen* Selection	C. Fischer
Copland	"Waltz" from *Billy the Kid*	Boosey & Hawkes
Handel-Harris	Largo	Bourne
Schuman	New England Triptych ("When Jesus Wept")	Merion
Wagner	"Prize Song", *Die Meistersinger*	C. Fischer

Difficult

Borodin	On the Steppes of Central Asia	G. Schirmer
Saint-Saëns	Danse Macabre	C. Fischer
Weber	Overture to *Oberon*	C. Fischer

BAND

Easy

Bach	Sixteen Chorales	G. Schirmer
Bach-Mairs	Christ Lay in Bonds of Death	Bourne
Dillon, arr.	Greensleeves	Hansen
Erickson	Norwegian Folk Song Suite	Bourne
Handel-Anderson	Song of Jupiter ("Where'er You Walk")	Mills
Haydn-Brahms-Tolmage	Chorale—St. Antoni	Staff
Ortone, arr.	Londonderry Air	Pro Art
Sibelius-Goldman	Onward, Ye Peoples	Galaxy

Medium

Christiansen	First Norwegian Rhapsody	Witmark
Handel-Leidzen	Care Selve	Associated
Humperdinck-Fitzgerald	*Hansel and Gretel* Selections	Summy-Birchard
Mozart-Beeler	Alleluia, *Exultate Jubilate*	G. Schirmer
Rimsky-Korsakov	Hymn to the Sun	C. Fischer
Schuman, Wm.	Chester, Overture for Band	Merion
Schuman, Wm.	When Jesus Wept	Merion
Strauss-Davis	Allerseelen	Ludwig
Strauss-Davis	Zueignung	Ludwig

Difficult

Borodin-Barnes	On the Steppes of Central Asia	Shapiro-Bernstein
Dukas	The Sorcerer's Apprentice	C. Fischer
Respighi	The Pines of the Appian Way	Ricordi
Stravinsky	Circus Polka	Associated
Weber	Invitation to the Dance	C. Fischer

Special Experiences for Vocal Music Classes

Tonal color should also be a concern of singers. A better understanding of timbre may be developed in choral rehearsals through allowing the students to:

1. Experiment with the various timbres possible with voices.

2. Make a list of words used to imitate other sounds (e.g., Nagler's *Serenade in Snow*).

3. Find words commonly used in instrumental music which are helpful in achieving certain kinds of vocal tone. (e.g., "Sing with rosin on the bows," "sing this chordal melody like a fanfare," "sound like muted strings," "boys, sing this majestic passage with authority, as if you were playing trombones," or "let's get a brassy sound here.")

4. Discuss onomatopoeia.

5. Sing songs (with younger groups) which imitate the sounds of the instruments (e.g., *The Orchestra Song, The Instruments Charm Me*, or *Old King Cole*).

6. Listen to an instrumental performance of songs that appear also in orchestral or band compositions.

Tchaikovsky	A Legend
Arensky	Variations on a Theme by Tchaikovsky
Bach	Chorales
Bach	Chorale Preludes
Bach	Jesu, Joy of Man's Desiring
Beethoven	Joyful, Joyful, We Adore Thee
Beethoven	Ninth Symphony
Brahms	Gaudeamus Igitur
Brahms	Academic Festival Overture
Dvořák	Goin' Home
Dvořák	New World Symphony
Haydn	Austrian Hymn
Haydn	Emperor Quartet
Sibelius	O Morn of Beauty
Sibelius	Finlandia

7. Sing songs which utilize instrumental accompaniments or obbligato parts for instruments or which imitate instrumental timbres.

Alcock	Voix Celestes	Chappell
Anderson	Gatatumba (Andalusian Carol)	G. Schirmer

Bach	Jesu, Joy of Man's Desiring (with flute or recorder and organ or orchestra)	G. Schirmer
Bach	Jesu, nun sei ge preiset (3 trumpets, timpani)	R. King
Bach	"Sleepers Wake", Cantata 140 Chorus No. 2 (oboe and organ or orchestra)	Novello
Barthelson, arr.	Bagpipe Carol	Skidmore
Barthelson, arr.	Joseph Dearest, Joseph Mine (violin or flute and cello obbligato)	Skidmore
Besly	The Shepherds Had An Angel (Eng. horn)	G. Schirmer
Brahms	Geistliches Wiegenlied, Op. 91 (viola)	International
Czech-Davis	Carol of the Drum (snare drum) (also pub. for orchestra, arr. Wright)	Wood
Dengler-Walton	Johnny Schmoker	Presser
Elgar	The Snow (violin)	Novello
Frackenpohl	Shepherds, Rejoice (3 trumpets, 3 trombones, baritone, tuba)	R. King
French Carol	Slumber Song of the Infant Jesus (flute)	Summy-Birchard
Kodály	Christmas Dance of the Shepherds	Presser
Kodály	Soldier's Song (with trumpet and drum)	Boosey & Hawkes
Krone, arr.	Pat-A-Pan	Kjos
Leontovich-Wilhousky	Carol of the Bells	C. Fischer
Mendelssohn	On Wings of Song (harp)	Bourne
Nagler	Serenade in Snow	G. Schirmer
Pinkham	Angelus Ad Pastores (brass)	R. King
Schuman, arr.	The Orchestra Song	G. Schirmer
Wilson, arr.	Fum, Fum, Fum	Bourne
Wilson, arr.	The Orchestra	SHM
Winslow, arr.	Mary's Lullaby (violin, clarinet, cello obbligato)	Wood

FILMS

Appalachian Spring	Rembrandt, Contemporary
Beethoven Sonata (demonstration of construction and brief history of the horn)	Contemporary
Colors in Music	NET

Elements of Composition	NET
Forms of Instrumental Music	Coronet
Instruments of the Band and Orchestra	Coronet
Instruments of the Orchestra	Contemporary
Instruments of the Symphony Orchestra	Jam Handy
Introducing the Brasses	NET
Introducing the Woodwinds	NET
Meet the Instruments of the Symphony Orchestra	Bowmar
Music of Williamsburg	Modern
Pacific 231	McGraw-Hill
Percussion: The Pulse of Music	NET
Science and the Orchestra	McGraw-Hill
Hearing the Orchestra	
Exploring the Instruments	
Looking at Sounds	
The Changing Voice	FSU
The String Choir	EBF

RECORDINGS

Adventures in Music Series	RCA Victor
Bowmar Orchestral Library (11 albums)	Bowmar
Britten, *Variations and Fugue on a Theme by Purcell*	London
The Complete Orchestra	Mus. Ed. Record Corp.
The Composer and His Orchestra	Mercury
First Chair	Columbia
Instruments of the Orchestra	Columbia
Instruments of the Orchestra	RCA-J. W. Pepper
The Orchestra	Capitol
Rimsky-Korsakov, *Scheherazade*	Columbia
Stravinsky, *Petrouchka*	RCA

BIBLIOGRAPHY

Baines, Anthony, editor. *Musical Instruments Through the Ages.*
Baines, Anthony. *Woodwind Instruments and Their History.*
Carse, Adam. *Musical Wind Instruments.*
Carse, Adam. *The Orchestra in the XVIII Century.*
Culver, C. A. *Musical Acoustics.*
Donington, Robert. *The Instruments of Music.*
Dorf, R. H. *Electronic Musical Instruments.*
Kinsky, Georg, and others. *History of Music in Pictures.*
Kirby, Percival Robson. *The Kettle-Drums.*
Richardson, E. G. *The Acoustics of Orchestral Instruments and of the Organ.*
Sachs, Curt. *The History of Musical Instruments.*
Terry, Charles Sanford. *Bach's Orchestra.*

    (Detailed bibliographical information on these items will be found in the bibliography at the end of the book.)

Content Area 2

FORM OR DESIGN IN MUSIC

Each of the constituent elements of music discussed in Content Area 1 has its own structure. In like manner, combinations of them have characteristic structures.

In this publication, "Form in Music" and "Design in Music" or "Musical Design" are used synonymously to denote the interrelationships and interactions which exist among the constituent elements of music. These terms refer to relationships among the constituent elements within a composition rather than to the design of the composition as a whole.[2] Form *in* music relates to the syntax of the musical language. It defines the pattern of its musical procedures.

If form is equated with the interrelationships and interactions which exist among the constituent elements of music, it necessarily is inclusive of them. It therefore follows that an understanding of form requires an understanding of each of the constituent elements that is interrelated. In this sense, an understanding of form is the master key that unlocks the door to musical understanding. This fact has been recognized and stated by numerous leaders in music education.

In this connection the late James L. Mursell wrote:

> Music undoubtedly does have great emotion-rousing effectiveness and, indeed, a highly specific emotional impact. But it has such an effect not simply because of its content but because of its organization. Without organization, music would simply cease to be. So, progressively more adequate grasp of musical organization is the very heart and center of progressively more adequate appreciation.[3]

---

[2] See the two definitions of form in the *Harvard Dictionary of Music*. The second of these which treats of form as "the scheme of organization" is dealt with in a number of the other content areas, specifically: 1A—Rhythm; 6—Historical Considerations; 9—Types of Musical Performance; and 10—Relationship of Music to Other Disciplines in the Humanities.

[3] James L. Mursell, "Growth Processes in Music Education." *Basic Concepts in Music Education.* 57th Yearbook, Part I, National Society for the Study of Education. (Chicago: University of Chicago Press, 1958), p. 152.

Oleta Benn speaks of the importance of form in these words:

The development of susceptibility to form is the central purpose of all those who would have their students hear or produce music musically. Music is a form of communication which man has developed into an art of the highest order, using the unique medium of sound. We are compelled to teach to others the forms and symbols which will permit them to understand its meaning. Such meaning is not conveyed through formlessness. It cannot be discerned, therefore, by those who fail to recognize the order of its statement. In this context, by form we are really speaking of design. It includes all those effects of sound which composers use to make their musical ideas known to others, the final organization of which may result in the simplest of four-measure rote songs or the grandeur and complexity of a symphony.[4]

In stating that "The ability to detect form is the heart of musical education," Harry S. Broudy wrote as follows:

There is a level of listening on which one simply hears these elements come and go and responds to them with feelings of pleasantness or unpleasantness. It is something like enjoying the changing colors of a kaleidoscope. . . . But to stop at this level of listening is to sadden the hearts of the musical composer, performer, and educator. For the whole purpose of composition is to weave these materials into a pattern that has continuity and dramatic structure. . . . Let us call this continuity and structure the form or the design of the composition. . . .

In music, as in all art, form makes or breaks the work with regard to both the composer and the listener. Unless the listener detects form, he is limited to the most rudimentary level of appreciation, namely, the apprehension of the aesthetic qualities of isolated tones and phrases. Hence, as we shall have many occasions to note, the ability to detect form is the heart of musical education.[5]

A composition derives organic unity through repetition of some of its elements. It derives variety and contrast as one or more of them is altered while the others are repeated identically. The recognition of these relationships—of the way in which one part of a composition is derived from, but is different than, an earlier part—is an indispensable factor

[4] Oleta Benn, "A Message for New Teachers." 57th Yearbook, Part I, op. cit., p. 341.

[5] Harry S. Broudy, "A Realistic Philosophy of Music Education." 57th Yearbook, Part I, op. cit., pp. 70-71.

in understanding the process through which a composition makes sense with itself. The musical design which results from this process is perceived as form *in* music. A few of the many ways in which relationships among the elements of a theme can be varied in the design of a composition are illustrated on the following pages.

These examples illustrate in musical terms the processes through which unity and contrast are simultaneously achieved in compositions of various periods, forms, styles, and media of performance. The implications for the selection of a repertoire for listening, and in some cases for performing, are obvious.

Experiences All Music Classes Should Provide

In order to examine the formal aspects of a piece of music in the detailed manner which will be presented on pages 49 to 53, students will need to have opportunities to:

1. Develop an understanding of the distinction between form in music and forms of music through listening to much music and discussing it.

2. Recognize identical and contrasting phrases in folk and art songs both by ear and by observation of the musical notation.

3. Recognize tonal and rhythmic patterns repeated in identical or altered form by ear and by observation of the musical notation.

4. Investigate the sources of unity and contrast in a variety of musical compositions.

5. Hear and understand the contrast between contrapuntal textures and homophonic structures.

UNITY AND CONTRAST

It is important for the musically educated person to understand the processes through which unity and contrast are achieved in a composition. In William Schuman's *New England Triptych,* the third movement, "Chester," provides an excellent example for analysis that is essentially non-technical. Its basic theme can be sung. Schuman's setting of this theme can be listened to by means of a recording. It can be played by a superior high school orchestra or band.

The following pages outline experiences through which pupils can investigate and discover the structure of this music. They were prepared for a course in which the primary activity is listening, but pupils in bands and orchestras can simply play the particular passages designated for listening and, by comparing their structure analytically, achieve the same result.

The analyses given in the succeeding pages are somewhat detailed. This material is intended to be suggestive of the kinds of things that can be done with numerous other compositions.

A theme may have a characteristic rhythmic pattern (A^1) which may be repeated with varying melodic material (A^2) and (A^3) as in the measures quoted from the second movement of Beethoven's *Symphony No. 8* (Example 1).

EXAMPLE 1

This type of relationship frequently appears in songs. For example, it may be found in "The Marines' Hymn," "The Star-Spangled Banner," "All Creatures of Our God and King," "O God Our Help in Ages Past," "Auld Lang Syne," and "America, the Beautiful."

The characteristic melodic pattern of a theme may be repeated with changes in the rhythmic pattern, the meter, and the tempo as in *Till Eulenspiegel* by Richard Strauss (Example 2). See also the fourth movement of Beethoven's *Symphony No. 9,* measures 140-143 and 655-658, and the *Variations on Pop Goes the Weasel,* by Lucien Cailliet.

EXAMPLE 2

The melodic contour of a theme may be retained while its harmonic structure, rhythmic design, and tempo are changed, as shown in the measures from William Schuman's "Chester" (Example 3).

EXAMPLE 3

This type of relationship may be found in numerous songs including "The Wasted Serenade," by Brahms and "O Tannenbaum." Or, observe the way Bach treats the chorale melodies in the verses of his cantatas; e.g., *Christ Lay in the Bonds of Death* (verses V and VII).

The essential design of the elements of a theme may be repeated with a change of tone color, as in "The Conversation of the Beauty and the Beast," from the *Mother Goose Suite* of Maurice Ravel (Example 4).

EXAMPLE 4

Permission for reprint granted by Durand et Cie, Paris, copyright owners, and Elkan-Vogel Co., Inc., Philadelphia, agents.

Students should be encouraged to compare the middle section of *Finlandia* by Sibelius as played by the woodwinds with the repetition of the passage played by the strings. There are two recordings of "Chester" by William Schuman. One is for band; the other, for orchestra. Students can listen to both and discuss the contrasting instrumental effects. A similar procedure can be followed with the *Little Fugue in g minor* by Bach, using two recordings, one played on the organ and the other played by an orchestra. Interesting contrasts of tone color may be found in the *Song of Jupiter* by Handel-Anderson, which is a setting for band of the aria, "Where'er You Walk."

The tonal relationships of a theme may remain the same while being lengthened in time. This aspect of form in music is called *augmentation*. It is demonstrated by Aaron Copland in *Appalachian Spring* (Example 5).

EXAMPLE 5

Original ♩ = 80

Ob

Measure 497 *mp*

Augmentation

Tbn
Va

Measure 514 *mp dolce*

© 1945 by Aaron Copland; Boosey & Hawkes, Inc., sole licensees.
Reprinted by permission.

Augmentation may be found in numerous compositions. Among them are the *American Salute* by Morton Gould, the "Prelude" to *Hansel and Gretel* by Humperdinck, and the *Great Gate at Kiev* by Mussorgsky. The augmentation should be recognized by students who hear recordings of these compositions and by members of instrumental organizations that may be rehearsing them.

The melodic contour of a theme may remain the same while being shortened in time. This aspect of form is called *diminution* and is demonstrated by another quotation from "Chester" (Example 6). In this example, in addition to the diminution there is a change in tempo. This increases the *effect* of the diminution.

EXAMPLE 6

Religioso ♩ = 72

Wwds

Measure 1   *p dolce legato*

Allegro Vivo ♩ = 160

Wwds

Measure 46   *f*

Copyright 1957, Merion Music, Inc.
Used by permission.

Diminution may be found also in the *Russian Chorale and Overture* by Isaac, and students who are performing this music should identify it.

A theme, or a pattern from it, may be turned upside down. This aspect of form in music, called *inversion,* may be observed in the first movement of Brahms' *Symphony No. 3* (Example 7). See also measures 1-5 and 74-78 of the "Chaconne" (allegro moderato) from the *First Suite in Eb for Military Band* by Gustav Holst.

EXAMPLE 7

A tonal pattern in a melody or theme may be repeated successively at either higher or lower pitches. This aspect of form in music is called a *sequence.* Bach provides many examples of this, as in his *Little Fugue in g minor,* (Example 8). Sequences may be found in many songs: for example, "America," "O Tannenbaum," "If I Could Fly," and "San Sereni."

EXAMPLE 8

TEXTURE IN MUSIC

The various ways in which the voices or parts within a composition may be combined result in characteristic textures of tone. There are, basically, two types of textures in music. Music which consists of several melodically independent "voices" has a *polyphonic* (many-voiced) texture. The melodies move independently, but there is coherence in their relationship.

Music which consists of one important melody supported by other subservient voices which create a harmonic or chordal background has a *homophonic* texture. The supporting voices may be organized in a rhythmic pattern unlike the predominating melody as in the second movement of Beethoven's *Symphony No. 7* (Example 9).

EXAMPLE 9

Measure 150

Or, the supporting voices may be organized in a rhythmic pattern which is essentially the same as that of the primary melody. See "Be Not Afraid" from the oratorio *Elijah* by Felix Mendelssohn (Example 10).

EXAMPLE 10

In contrast to the homophonic textures mentioned above, the interweaving of melodic lines creates textures that are polyphonic in nature. If, for example, an identical melody is presented by several voices entering at different points in time, a *canonic* texture is created. A more complex application of this same principle of organization is the basis for the opening section of a composition called a *fugue*. (See material under the heading *Special Experiences for Instrumental Music Classes*.)

DEVELOPMENT OF A MUSICAL CONCEPT

The development of conceptual understandings as a way of teaching has much to recommend it in the area of music. A lesson using this approach is presented in detail in the firm belief that all students must at some time in their schooling be taught to study a piece of music in this way if they are to realize the outcomes of Chapter II, especially numbers I, IV, and XI. One concept to be taught is: *When a composition is based on a single theme, it may achieve unity through the repetition of certain elements of its design, and contrast through the alteration of other elements.*

The materials to be used include a score of "Chester", Overture for Band by William Schuman (Merion Music, Inc.), a recording of the same composition (Decca 8633-Goldman), and a recording of "Chester" as sung by the Robert Shaw Chorale in the album, "This Is My Country" (Victor LM 2662). The song would also be notated on the chalkboard in a lower key for singing (Example 11).

EXAMPLE 11   Billings

Let ty-rants shake their i - - - - ron rod, And slav - 'ry clank ——— her gal - - - ling chains. We'll fear them not, we ——— trust ——— in God, New Eng-land's God ——— for - ev - - er reigns.

Experiences Through Which the Concept Will Be Developed.—The class will:

A. Listen to the recording of measures 1 through 37, while following the notation of the song on the chalkboard.

B. Sing the song to develop familiarity with the theme.

C. Discover the prominent characteristics of the theme through singing, listening, and discussion.

1. The melody moves predominantly in a scalewise manner with occasional intervals of the *third, fourth,* and *fifth.*

2. The melody is organized into four phrases of four measures each.

a. The first three phrases start with the rhythmic pattern ♩ ♩ ♩ but the beginning of the fourth phrase is characterized by a distinctive rhythmic figure: ♩. ♪ ♩ ♩ . The rhythm of the last two measures of every phrase is identical.

b. The melodic pattern of the first two measures of the first phrase appears in the middle of the third phrase.

3. The theme (as heard in the first 16 measures) is presented in a four-part *homophonic texture* with the first two phrases ending on the *dominant* harmony, and the last two phrases ending on the *tonic.*

D. Listen to the recording of the entire composition to discover the most obvious characteristics of the music as a whole. During the playing of the record the teacher will point out those parts of the theme (notated on the chalkboard) which are most obvious in the music.

1. In the beginning the theme is played twice, first by the woodwinds and then by the brasses.

2. Almost immediately, the theme is played again by the woodwinds at a very fast tempo. The last two measures of this statement are repeated many times with rhythmic changes. The melodic pattern sounds the same but the rhythm is different.

3. The first two phrases of the theme are played with rhythmic alterations, including syncopation, while the theme itself is altered by the addition of certain notes.

4. The entire theme is varied melodically, rhythmically, and harmonically. Only its general contour is maintained.

5. Just before the coda, the third phrase of the melody is lengthened in time (*augmentation*).

E. Hear, analyze, identify, and discuss numerous passages in which one aspect of the theme is identical with its original statement, and one or more aspects are different. Repeated hearings are essential. The discussion should include descriptions of the ways in which one aspect of the theme may be identical with its original statement and one or more aspects may be different; i.e., the tonal pattern may be the same and the rhythm pattern different, or vice versa. Following are some examples:

1. The melody is played by the woodwinds (measures 46 through 61) approximately four times as fast as it was heard originally. The time values of the notes have been cut in half—*diminution*—and the tempo has been approximately doubled. (See Example 5.) This is accompanied by a *dissonant chord* (Example 12) repeated throughout many measures as a rhythmic *pulse* by the brasses.

EXAMPLE 12

Accompanying Chord

2. Measures 101 through 122 consist of rhythmic, melodic, and harmonic variations of the first two phrases of the theme. In what ways is this true? See Example 13, in which the first phrase of the theme has been transposed to Eb.

3. In the woodwinds, from measures 154 through 171, the contour of the melody is retained, but its harmony is dif-

EXAMPLE 13

ferent and its intervals are changed. In the melody, some tones are deleted while others are inserted (Example 14).

EXAMPLE 14

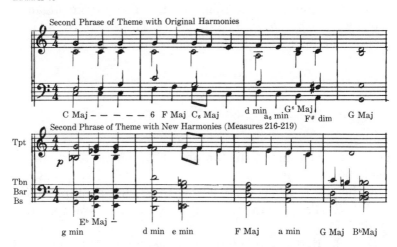

4. The first and second phrases of the original melody are played by the brasses in measures 212 through 219, but the harmonies are altered (Example 15).

EXAMPLE 15

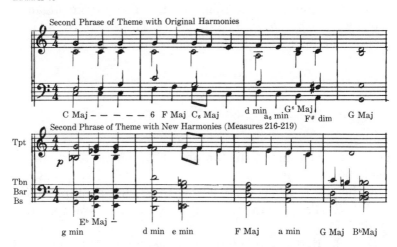

5. Measures 228 (Example 16) is derived from measures 13 and 14 of the original theme. Through listening, observation of the notation written on the chalkboard, and discussion, the class should discover that the melody of measure 228 seems to move twice as fast as it does in the subsequent two measures. In relation to the fourth phrase of the original theme, measure 228 is in *diminution*, for the time values of the notes are reduced by half. Although the

time values of measures 229 and 230 are the same as in the original theme, in relation to measure 228 they have the effect of *augmentation.*

EXAMPLE 16

6. The coda is based on the first two measures of the theme and consists mostly of rhythmic variations.

Special Experiences for Nonselective Music Classes

As in the previous section, a detailed lesson plan such as might be used with an unselected class in music will be presented (see pages 54 to 59). In order to benefit from such study, students will need to have had experience in:

1. Recognizing by ear and notation, (a) melodies which are repeated with altered rhythm, (b) rhythms which are repeated with altered melodies, (c) melodies which are repeated with altered harmonies, and (d) melodies which are repeated with altered tempo.

2. Recognizing by ear and notation such compositional techniques as augmentation, diminution, inversion, canon, and fugue.

3. Listening to and analyzing compositions in theme and variation form. Students should be assisted in inquiring as to which musical elements remain the same, which are varied, and how they are varied. Compositions which might be used for this include Haydn's *Quartet,* Op. 76, No. 3 (Emperor), 2nd Movement; Brahms' *Variations on a Theme by Haydn;* Haydn's *Symphony No. 94* (Surprise), 2nd Movement; Schubert's *Symphony No. 2,* 2nd Movement; Schubert's *Quintet,* Op. 114 (Trout), 4th Movement; Mozart's A Major *Piano Sonata,* 1st Movement; Fauré's *Theme and*

Variations; Cailliet's *Variations on Pop Goes the Weasel;* Dohnanyi's *Variations on a Nursery Theme.*

4. Inquiring into the reasons why form in music is inclusive of all other musical elements.

The following material provides an analysis of the third movement of *Symphony No. 2* by Brahms and the second movement of Beethoven's *Symphony No. 8.* If the students can come to understand the relationships of design that are set forth for the teacher in this material, they will have made substantial progress in understanding form in music. Experiences which will lead to this understanding include thoughtful listening to the music; recognizing by ear important patterns that are repeated, whether in identical or altered form; observing the notation of these patterns; analyzing the similarities and differences that exist among them; and rehearing the music to identify these forms by ear.

BRAHMS—*Symphony No. 2* IN D MAJOR (THIRD MOVEMENT)

A. This movement is written in the particular rondo form in which the first section appears at least three times, separated by other material. The sections can easily be identified because of their contrasting tempos. Comparatively speaking, the sections may be described as slow, fast, slow, fast, slow. The design of the movement may be designated by the letters A-B-A-C-A, although it should be pointed out that parts of C are derived from B.

B. The movement begins with a simple, lyric melody in three-four meter introduced by the oboe (Example 17).

EXAMPLE 17

From this theme grows another, played in two parts by the oboes. It is continued by the flutes and clarinets. There is a complete halt, and then a return to Example 17.

C.   The second section (B) (Presto in two-four meter) is introduced by the strings which are then joined by the winds (Example 18). It is built on Example 17 (notes common to the two passages are circled). This is followed by a

EXAMPLE 18

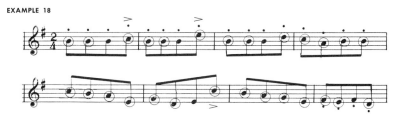

tune played in martial style by the strings, woodwinds and French horns (Example 19). Although Example 19 is *not* an inversion of Example 17, it gives the effect of an inversion, for where Example 17 moves upward, Example 19 moves downward, and vice versa.

EXAMPLE 19

col 8va

Tonal Pattern from Example 17   Tonal Pattern from Example 19

D.   Following Section B, Section A returns in modified form. Its melody is Example 17, played by the first oboe and then by the first flute. A pattern taken from Example 17 is then played by the strings.

E.   The fourth section (C) begins with a descending scale passage played by the strings. Its tempo (Presto in three-eight meter) is the same as that of Section B. Woodwinds then play in three-eight meter the pattern of Example

19 which was originally played in two-four meter (Example
20). Repetition of patterns in different meters is one of the
chief characteristics of the movement. This passage is related
to Example 19 which provides the link between Sections C
and B. It is in this sense that some teachers may prefer to
designate Section C as B[1].

EXAMPLE 20   Later

F.   At the end of this section there is a transition passage
in which woodwinds predominate and the tempo gradually
becomes slower.

G.   The fifth section (A) follows with Example 17 in F#
Major instead of in G as at the beginning of the movement.

H.   After a complete stop there is a repetition of Example 17 as it was heard at the beginning. This is inter-
rupted by a particularly beautiful melody played by high
strings, after which woodwinds predominate to the end of
the movement.

BEETHOVEN—*Symphony No. 8*, IN F MAJOR (SECOND
MOVEMENT)

The second movement (Allegretto scherzando) is written
in two-four meter and scored for small orchestra without
trumpets or timpani.

A.   The opening theme, based primarily on the repetition
of a three-note pattern (Figure A), is played by the first
violins (Example 21).

EXAMPLE 21

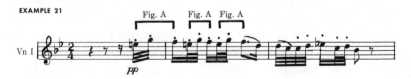

B.   The theme is accompanied by steady, staccato, six-
teenth-notes played by woodwinds and horns (Example 22).

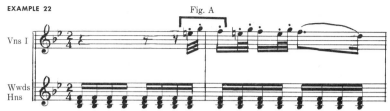

EXAMPLE 22   Fig. A

Vns I

Wwds
Hns

C. The use of the three-note pattern both rhythmically and melodically is continued throughout the movement and is the key to its understanding. Immediately the cellos and string basses play the rhythm of Figure A with a different melody (Example 23). At other points in the movement the original rhythmic pattern of Figure A is heard with different melodies (Examples 24 and 25).

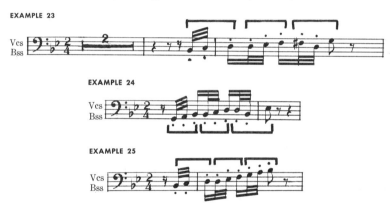

EXAMPLE 23

Vcs
Bss

EXAMPLE 24

Vcs
Bss

EXAMPLE 25

Vcs
Bss

D. The second important theme (Example 26) seems to have a somewhat different character than the first. Probably this is due to the duration of the two dotted eighth-notes which are longer than most notes heard up to this point. The first three notes have the rhythmic and melodic pattern of Figure A.

EXAMPLE 26

Fig. A   Fig. A Inverted

Vns I

Fig. A Inverted

E. In the third, fourth, and fifth notes of Example 26 the tonal pattern of Figure A is inverted (turned upside down). Notes 5, 6, 7 are also an inversion of the tonal pattern of Figure A.

F. Later the principal theme is heard again in varied form (Example 27). This version of the theme is characterized by repeated notes.

EXAMPLE 27

G. Example 26 returns in a different key and at one point is heard in the form of a canon (exact imitation), starting with clarinets and bassoons in octaves answered by flutes, oboes, and upper strings (Example 28).

EXAMPLE 28

H. Sudden loud attacks followed by soft passages are heard throughout the movement and are therefore one of its prominent characteristics (Example 29).

EXAMPLE 29

I. In the coda, Beethoven continues to use the three-note pattern and the sudden changes of dynamics. The final three measures start pianissimo and build to a fortissimo.

Other compositions for which similar procedures are appropriate include the following: Bach, *Passacaglia and Fugue,* in c minor; Samuel Barber, *Symphony No. 1,* in One Movement; Beethoven, *Symphony No. 3,* in E Flat (Eroica), Fourth Movement; Brahms, *Variations on a Theme by*

Haydn; Hanson, *Symphony No. 2* (Romantic), any move-ment; Harris, *Symphony No. 3;* Haydn, *Symphony No. 94,* in G Major, Second Movement; Mendelssohn, *Symphony No. 4,* in A Major (Italian), First Movement; Mozart, *Symphony No. 35,* in D Major (Haffner), First Movement; Prokofiev, *Classical Symphony,* First Movement; Schubert, *Symphony No. 2,* in B Flat Major, Second Movement; Schu-bert, *Symphony No. 5,* in B Flat Major, First Movement; and R. Strauss, *Till Eulenspiegel.*

Special Experiences for Instrumental Music Classes

It is important for young people who participate in bands and orchestras in the secondary schools to understand the structure of the music they are performing. Through such understanding, their performance becomes more knowledge-able and it can reveal the design of the music more clearly to the listener.

The following material related to the *Little Fugue in g minor* by J. S. Bach is included as one example of the ex-periences through which young people in performing groups can come to understand contrapuntal textures in music they may be performing. Through experiences such as those out-lined, the rehearsal of the performing group becomes in fact the study of music.

DEVELOPMENT OF MUSICAL CONCEPTS

Concepts.—When one voice or instrument states a theme, then continues with another melody while a second voice or instrument restates the first theme a fifth higher or a fourth lower, and when this procedure continues through three or four entrances of the original theme (subject), *the begin-ning of a fugue may be created.*

As each new "voice" enters with the subject, the preceding "voice" continues with new material in counterpoint to it. If this material attains importance throughout the fugue, it may be referred to as a countersubject.

Statements of the subject may be separated by interludes of free counterpoint. These are called episodes. *They may contain melodic or rhythmic patterns derived from the subject or countersubject.*

The materials to be used include the orchestration of Bach's *Fugue in g minor* ("The Little"), made by Lucien Cailliet (Carl Fischer, Inc.); a recording of the same (Victor LE 1009, Adventures in Music, Grade 6 Volume I, Side 1); and the subject and countersubject notated on the chalkboard.

Experiences Through Which the Concepts Will Be Developed.—The orchestra will:

A.   Listen to a recording of the entire composition, while reading from the individual parts, to discover (a) the most obvious characteristics of the music as a whole; (b) those musical details which are discernible at a first hearing.

1.   There is one principal theme, known as the subject (Example 30), that reappears frequently throughout the composition. The statements of the subject are sometimes interspersed with passages that are contrasting in melody and rhythm. Several different melodies can be heard at the same time. Near the end, the composition rises in pitch and in volume to a magnificent climax.

EXAMPLE 30

2.   At the beginning of the fugue, the subject is heard four times at successively lower pitches played by the following instruments: (a) the first clarinet; (b) the English horn and second clarinet; (c) the bass clarinet, bassoons, and violas; and (d) the lower woodwinds and strings.

3.   After each voice has stated the subject, it continues with new material called the countersubject, while

the next voice enters with the subject. The first statement of the countersubject is found in measures 6 through 10 (Example 31).

EXAMPLE 31

B. Listen again to measures 23 to 26 (Example 32). Discuss the music to discover that:

    1. It is different from the subject.

    2. The two upper voices imitate each other. The two lower melodies are also imitative.

    3. This passage (a) leads to a re-statement of the subject, (b) functions as an interlude between statements of the subject, and (c) may be called an episode.

EXAMPLE 32

C. Rehearse measures 1 through 10.

    1. Listen to the first clarinet to discover that the first measure of the subject, being essentially chordal, serves to establish the key of g minor (Example 33) and that meas-

EXAMPLE 33

EXAMPLE 34

Measure 3

Measure 4

ure 4 is a varied repetition of measure 3 (Example 34). Replay and compare these two measures. Listen to the clarinet
in measure 6, the first measure of the countersubject, and
observe that this is an altered repetition of measure 5 on a
higher pitch level (Example 35). Replay and compare

EXAMPLE 35

Measure 5

Measure 6

these two measures. Note also that the pitches at the end
of the subject are the same as those of notes 2 through 10
(Example 36). The time values are shorter. For this reason,
the end of the subject sounds like a *diminution* of its beginning, though this is not strictly so. Replay and compare
these two fragments of the subject.

EXAMPLE 36

Measure 1

Measure 4

2. Listen while the first clarinet plays measures 1
through 5 (subject). Listen while the English horn and the
second clarinet play measures 6 through 10 (answer). Discuss the similarities and differences between these two pas-

sages to bring out that (a) the melodies are the same; (b) the rhythm is the same; and (c) the pitch level is different, measures 6 through 10 being a fourth lower.

3. Listen to measures 6 through 10 as played by the woodwinds. Discover that two melodic lines are moving counter to each other, creating a texture known as *counter-point*. Discover that the English horn and second clarinet are playing the melody of the subject while the flute and first clarinet play the countersubject. Note that the first measure of the countersubject (measure 6) is an altered repetition of measure 5 on a higher pitch level. (See brackets A and A[1] in the Examples 30 and 31.)

D. Rehearse the rest of the composition to develop understandings related to the structure of a fugue through listening, discussion, and non-technical analysis.

1. Listen to the French horns play the subject (in B♭ Major) from measures 34 through 38, and the high woodwinds and violins play the subject (in c minor) from measures 52 through 56 to discover that later statements of the subject are in different keys.

2. Listen to the flutes play measure 7 and then listen to the violas and cellos play measures 23 and 24 (Example 37). Discover that the sequences in this passage are derived from the countersubject (measure 7).

EXAMPLE 37

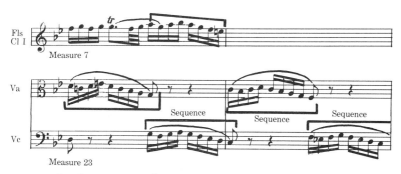

3. Listen in order to the passages in Example 38; i.e., measure 11 with the upbeat by the clarinet; measures 38, 39

by the French horn; and measures 40, 41 by violins, clarinet
I, oboes, and flutes. Analyze and discuss these passages to
bring out the fact that measures 38 and 41 are related to
measure 11.

EXAMPLE 38

4. Compare the episode (measures 23 through 25)
played by the strings with that (measures 47 through 51)
played by the woodwinds. Discover through listening and
discussion that they are based on the same thematic material
but are performed at different pitch levels.

Academically talented students should be encouraged to
peruse one or more of the following books:

Davison, Archibald T. *Bach and Handel: The Consummation of the
Baroque in Music.*

Geiringer, Karl. *The Bach Family: Seven Generations of Creative
Genius.*

Geiringer, Karl. *The Music of the Bach Family.*

Grew, Eva Mary and Sydney Grew. *Bach.*

Hindemith, Paul. *Johann Sebastian Bach: Heritage and Obligation.*

Schweitzer, Albert. *J. S. Bach.* (2 vols.) Translated by Ernest
Newman.

Terry, Charles Sanford. *The Music of Bach.*

Reference is made to the settings for orchestra and band
of "Chester" by William Schuman for which material may
be found on pages 49-53 in the section headed *Experiences
All Music Classes Should Provide.* Superior performing
groups can profit greatly by rehearsing and analyzing this
music.

Other compositions through which similar learnings may be developed are as follows:

ORCHESTRA

Easy

Bach-Elliot	Prelude, Passacaglia, and Fugue	Wynn
Bach-Marcelli	Chorale and Fugue	C. Fischer
Haydn-Isaac	Andante, Symphony in G Major	C. Fischer
Sammartini-Scarmolin	Symphony in D Major	Ludwig

Medium

Dittersdorf-Schmid	Symphony in F Major	G. Schirmer
Haydn	Symphony No. 104	Associated

Difficult

Handel-Kindler	Prelude and Fugue in d minor	Mills
Haydn	Symphony No. 103	Associated
Schuman, Wm.	New England Triptych	Merion

BAND

Easy

Bach-Moehlmann	Prelude and Fugue in f minor	FitzSimons
Clementi-Isaac	Sonatina, Op. 36, No. 1	C. Fischer
Handel-Osterling	Aria and Fugue	Ludwig

Medium

Bach-Moehlmann	Prelude and Fugue in B Flat Major	MPHC
Bach-Moehlmann	Prelude and Fugue in g minor	MPHC

Difficult

Bach-Moehlmann	Prelude and Fugue in d minor	FitzSimons
Handel-Maris	Prelude and Fugue in d minor	Marks
Holst	Suite No. 1 in E Flat, "Chaconne"	Boosey & Hawkes
Schuman, Wm.	"When Jesus Wept" from New England Triptych	Merion

Special Experiences for Vocal Music Classes

If young people participating in choral groups in the secondary schools are to become musically educated persons, they should develop an understanding of the meaning and structure of the music they rehearse and perform. Rehearsals can become truly educative to the extent that they include listening and analysis of the music that is rehearsed.

The material in the ensuing pages suggests experiences through which members of high school choirs can come to understand the structure of homophonic textures and of polyphonic textures and the differences between them. This material is suggestive of procedures that may be followed in developing similar learnings through other materials having similar structures. Through experiences such as those outlined, the rehearsal of the performing group becomes in fact the study of music.

DEVELOPMENT OF MUSICAL CONCEPTS

Concepts.—When one voice or instrument states a theme, then continues with another melody while a second voice or instrument restates the first theme a fifth higher or a fourth lower, and when this procedure continues through three or four entrances of the original theme (subject), *the beginning of a fugue may be created.*

As each new "voice" enters the subject, the preceding "voice" continues with new material in counterpoint to it. If this material attains importance throughout the fugue it may be referred to as a countersubject.

Statements of the subject may be separated by interludes of free counterpoint. These are called episodes. *They may contain melodic or rhythmic patterns derived from the subject or countersubject.*

The materials to be used include the vocal score to "And Then Shall Your Light Break Forth," from Mendelssohn's *Elijah,* and a recording of the same.

*Experiences Through Which the Concepts Will Be Developed.—*The choir will:

A. Listen to a recording of this composition, while reading from the vocal score, to discover:

1. The number of principal sections in this chorus as a whole.

2. The relationships that exist among the four voice parts in the main body of the composition.

B. Discuss points A.1. and A.2., after hearing the recording, to bring out the following facts:

1. There are three main sections in this composition. The first one is an introduction to the second. The third section is distinguished from the second by its essentially homophonic character. The second section is the main body of the composition.

2. In the second section the voice parts enter individually, each one singing the same phrase. The altos introduce the subject (or theme) in measures 18 through 23. It is then sung by (a) the sopranos a fifth higher than the altos, (b) the basses an octave lower than the altos, and (c) the tenor a fifth higher than the basses.

3. From this it may be noted that the relationship of the soprano part to the alto is duplicated in that of the tenor part to the bass. It may be noted that the alto and bass parts are identical as are also the soprano and tenor.

C. Sing the passage beginning with measure 18 and continuing through the conclusion of the tenor statement of the subject (measure 39). Altos and basses may sing it together in unison, and sopranos and tenors may sing their parts in unison, after which the entire section should be sung as written to provide aural recognition of the structure of these measures.

D. Listen again to the recording or sing from the beginning through to measure 39 for the purpose of discovering:

1. The contrast in structure between the first 17 measures and the ensuing measures.

2. The relationship of tempo and meter between the introduction and the fugal section.

E.   Discuss points D.1. and D.2. to bring out the following:

1.   The first part of the introduction is homophonic with all of the parts singing the same words in the same rhythm at the same time. In the second part of the introduction the voices imitate each other but only briefly.

2.   The tempo of the quarter notes in the introduction equals the tempo of the half notes when the altos enter with the subject of the main section.

F.   Listen again to the recording of the entire composition to note each entrance of the subject and the relative prominence of it in the total tonal texture and also the similarities and contrasts between section 2 and section 3.

G.   Discuss the number and sequence of the various entrances of the subject and what happened in the music that made it possible for them to be heard. The discussion pertaining to section 3 should take note of the following points:

1.   Much of it but not all of it is homophonic with the voices singing the same words and rhythm at the same time.

2.   Most of the third section is derived from the tonal and rhythmic nature of the principal subject.

H.   Examine the notation of the principal subject to discover that it is six measures long and that it consists of three distinct patterns of two measures each (Example 39).

1.   Note the rhythmic character of Figure A.

2.   Note the repeated intervals of the fourth in measures 3, 4, and 5.

EXAMPLE 39

Allegro. Doppio movimento ♩= 96

Lord our Cre – a – tor, how Ex – cel-lent Thy Name is in   all the   na–tions

I. Sing the passage beginning with measure 64 and continuing through measure 75 to discover where and in what ways Figures A, B, and D overlap each other (Example 40).

EXAMPLE 40

EXAMPLE 41

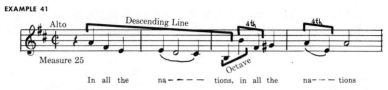

In all the   na – – – – tions, in all the   na – – – tions

J. Sing the alto part from measures 25 through 28 (Example 41). Rehearse and discuss this theme, known as the countersubject, to discover that:

1. Its movement is characterized by a descending line, an octave leap upward, and a pattern using the interval of a fourth.

2. It appears in each voice just after the succeeding voice has entered with the subject. The tenors, being last to enter, do not sing the countersubject. The alto sings the countersubject in measures 25 through 28, just after the soprano entrance. The sopranos sing the countersubject in measures 31 through 34, just after the bass entrance. The basses sing the countersubject in measures 36 through 39, just after the tenor entrance.

K. While rehearsing the remainder of the composition (from measure 41 to the end), discover through discussion

EXAMPLE 42

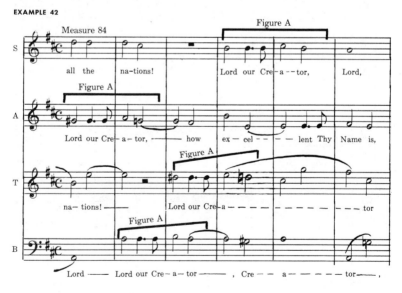

and non-technical analysis, the ways in which the parts are organized and related to the subject and the countersubject.

1. The complete subject appears (a) in the bass voice from measure 43 through 48 in f♯ minor, (b) in the alto voice from measure 51 through 56 in A Major, and (c) in the alto voice from measure 76 through 81 in D Major.

2. In measures 84 through 87 (Example 42), Figure A is sung by each voice beginning in consecutive measures. Thus, the voices crowd in upon one another. A passage in which this occurs is called *stretto*.

EXAMPLE 43

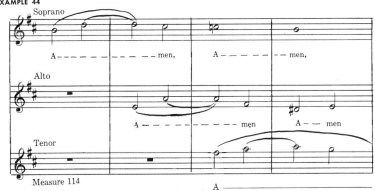

3. The final "Amen" section beginning with measure 114 (Example 44) is based on the "Amens" sung by the altos in measures 60 through 64 (Example 43).

EXAMPLE 44

4. In measures 118-119 the tenors sing an inversion of the "Amen" motive. This is answered by the basses in measures 122-123 (Example 45).

EXAMPLE 45

BIBLIOGRAPHY

Biancolli, Louis L. *The Analytical Concert Guide*.

Bruner, Jerome. *The Process of Education*.

Copland, Aaron. *What To Listen for in Music*.

Ferguson, Donald N. *Masterworks of the Orchestral Repertoire*.

Hartshorn, William C. *Music for the Academically Talented Student in the Secondary School*.

Hartshorn, William C. "The Role of Listening," *Basic Concepts in Music Education*.

Hopkins, Anthony. *Talking about Concertos*.

Hopkins, Anthony. *Talking about Symphonies*.

Landeck, Beatrice. "Basic Ideas in Elementary Music," *Music Educators Journal* (February-March, 1964), pp. 67-70.

Rossi, Nick, and Sadie Rafferty. *Music Through the Centuries*.

Toch, Ernst. *The Shaping Forces of Music*.

Tovey, Donald Francis. *Essays in Musical Analysis*.

Ulrich, Homer. *Symphonic Music*.

(Detailed bibliographical information on these items will be found in the bibliography at the end of the book.)

FILMS

Elements of Composition	NET
Extension of the Phrase	NET
Forms of Music	Coronet
Keyboard Conversation Series	NET
Music as a Language Series	NET
The Alphabet in Black	
The Alphabet in White	
Colors in Music	
An Essay in Sound	
Meter and Rhythm	
The Romantic Symphony	
The Six Basic Categories	
Musical Form Series	NET
The Fugue	
Passing Notes on Music Series	NET
Polyphony	
Sectional and Thematic Repetition	
Two Centuries of Symphony Series	NET
The Classical First Movement	
The Development of Musical Ideas	
Roy Harris Symphony No. 3	

Content Area 3

INTERPRETIVE ASPECTS OF MUSIC

Experiences All Music Classes Should Provide

In addition to the elements of music considered in Content Area 1, students need to understand that each performance of music is, in a sense, a *re-creation* in which the performer—the *re-creator* or interpreter—must deal with a number of variables (dynamics, tempo, phrasing, and choice of performing media) in order to achieve an artistic result. All students need experience in analyzing these interpretive aspects of music. They should be provided with opportunities to:

1. Examine the aesthetic triangle (composer, performer, listener) in order to determine the role that each plays in the arena of musical communication. Opportunity to talk with a local composer could be profitable.

2. Discuss the question "To what degree is the interpreter responsible to the composer?" An assembly program with a panel discussion involving a composer and a performer is a possibility here.

3. Compare through recordings the interpretation of a given work by several performers or conductors.

4. Observe techniques by which various conductors communicate their interpretive ideas to the players or singers.

5. Analyze the expressive potential in a 32-measure "pop" tune in comparison with that of a Beethoven sonata.

6. Develop an understanding of the broad subject of dynamics in music including the meanings and moods which are evoked by varying degrees of volume. The help of school performing groups should be enlisted for this purpose.

7. Discover how the use of different tempi will radically affect the character of the music. Once again, school performing groups should be utilized to help demonstrate this.

8. Examine phrasing in speech and compare it with musical phrasing. The study of plainsong and the recitative might be employed in this unit.

9. Study words, abbreviations, and signs with which composers designate expressive aspects of music: dynamics, tempo, phrasing, and mood. This study should be in relation to actual sounds that are heard and *never* mere memorization of the meaning of words and phrases.

10. Investigate the history of expression markings in conjunction with units prepared in relation to Content Area 6. Students should be aware of the absence or paucity of expression markings in the music before 1750 and consider the limitations in dynamic range and technical potential of early instruments. At the same time they should come to realize that music of the Renaissance and Baroque eras was most assuredly not devoid of expressive gradation.

11. Concentrate on the expressive qualities of music by attempting to find appropriate words (conventional markings or the students' own) to describe the mood of music to which they listen.

12. Listen to a given selection performed by different media (organ and orchestra, orchestra and band, instrument and voice, etc.), noting how the character of the music is changed.

Special Experiences for Nonselective Music Classes

Students in music classes in which performance of music is not a major objective may better understand the interpretive aspects of music if they are given the opportunity to:

1. Discover the tempo of their own heartbeats.

2. Learn to use the metronome.

3. Move at various tempi; i.e., largo, moderato, allegro, presto.

4. Experiment with the volume and speed controls on a record player. The importance of correct settings should be stressed and the reasons for this importance understood.

5. Examine the expression markings in their song books. What language (or languages) are used? Why? What abbreviations? What other marks of expression?

6. Sing songs in different tempi to observe the effects of speed upon what music communicates. The use of the tape recorder is recommended for this activity.

7. Conduct the class in the singing of familiar songs. Members of the class should evaluate each other's interpretation.

8. Study the relationship between the texts of songs and the manner in which the songs are sung. Special attention should be given to archaic and unfamiliar words.

9. Experiment with various styles of accompaniment on the autoharp in order to achieve a desired interpretation.

10. Apply the same high standards of interpretation to the playing of easy-to-play instruments as are traditionally applied to professional instruments.

11. Experiment in selecting instruments to accompany and to enrich a song.

12. Use the tape recorder in evaluating the interpretive phases of class performance.

13. Observe how different conductors interpret a given work. The use of the film *Conducting Good Music* (Encyclopaedia Britannica Films) is recommended.

14. Compare the expressive markings of the same song as it appears in two different publications.

15. Select a movement of a symphony (e.g., Scherzo from Tchaikovsky's *Fourth Symphony*) and compare several different recorded interpretations, noting particularly the tempo used and the actual metronomic speed of each.

16. Compare a recording of a song as done by a concert artist and by a "pop" singer (e.g., "He's Got the Whole World in His Hands," Marian Anderson and Laurie London).

Special Experiences for Instrumental Music Classes

Students in instrumental music classes should be encouraged to:

1. Learn background material appropriate to the interpretation of a composition—composer, historic significance, period, style, instrumentation, rhythm, melody, harmony, and form. This should apply to all music performed in class. (See the discussion of the use of Handel's *The Royal Fireworks Music* in *Music in the Senior High School.*[1])

2. Understand the role of posture and position and the vital importance of this "body-readiness" to the communication of a musical idea.

3. Learn to produce the special interpretive effects evoked by the spoken "word pictures" of the conductor (e.g., "Let's have more 'bite' on that attack, violins." "Very light, brass; barely 'kiss' each note.").

4. Develop a concept of tone. Instrumentalists should be encouraged to experiment with the different tone qualities possible on their instruments in order to be prepared to produce those which are most appropriate to a particular mood or style.

5. Develop the ability to follow the conductor's beat as he constantly varies the tempo and dynamics.

6. Increase their ability to hear their own sound in relation to the sounds of others. The use of the tape recorder is recommended for this purpose.

7. Develop the habit of observing all expressive designations in the music being rehearsed.

8. Experiment with various kinds of phrasing, analyzing why some are preferable to others.

9. Experiment with different tempi in order to discover what effect these variations have on what it is that the music ultimately communicates. These experiments need to be recorded and played back to the students.

10. Experiment with dynamic levels in like manner.

11. Develop the concept of the song approach to phrasing through the actual singing of their parts. The impor-

---

[1] *Music in the Senior High School.* (Washington, D.C.: Music Educators National Conference, 1954), pp. 51-54.

tance of breath to phrase length should be stressed. (e.g., A transcription of a Bach chorale might serve this purpose well; or, Brahms' *Third Symphony*, 3rd movement; Mendelssohn's *Nocturne*, Midsummer Night's Dream; Sibelius' *Finlandia;* Haydn's *London Symphony*, 1st movement; Borodin's *On the Steppes of Central Asia;* Mozart's *Quartet K421*, 3rd and 4th movements.)

12. Observe the changed effect when a melody is transcribed to a different key or played on another instrument.

Special Experiences for Vocal Music Classes

Students in vocal music classes should be motivated to:

1. Seek an understanding of a choral work before performing it. This will involve limited discussion of background material essential to its interpretation including: composer, poet, period, style, rhythm, melody, harmony, and form.

2. Analyze the text of a choral work as a clue to the mood, the dynamics, and the tempo.

3. Develop acute sensitivity to the conductor's beat. This skill may be developed during the vocalizing as the conductor constantly varies his beat.

4. Produce special musical effects evoked by the spoken "word pictures" of the conductor (e.g., "Can you get the hate of the crowd into that 'vah'?"—Dubois, *Seven Last Words*).

5. Develop the habit of observing all expressive designations in the music being rehearsed.

6. Understand the role and importance of posture and body readiness to breath control, tone quality, and the ability to communicate the spirit and flavor of the music.

7. Develop a concept of tone. Vocalists should be encouraged to think tone and to experiment with different qualities of singing tone in order to determine that which is most appropriate to the mood and style of a song.

8. Become familiar with the characteristic sound of such vocal combinations as the duet, trio, double trio, quartet,

double quartet, sextet, octet, SA choir, SSA choir, TB choir, TTBB choir, and SATB choir.

9. Develop the ability to listen to and hear their own sound in solo and as blend with other voices. The tape recorder is an invaluable tool in helping singers know their own voices.

10. Evaluate the recorded performances of professional choirs and compare interpretations with those of school organizations.

11. Compare the interpretations of an aria recorded by two leading opera singers. A similar comparison of recordings by professional choruses should also be part of the school singer's experience.

FILMS

Conducting Good Music	EBF
Music and Emotion	NET
Time in Music	NET

BIBLIOGRAPHY

Bodky, Erwin. *The Interpretation of Bach's Keyboard Works.*
Cooper, Grosvenor W., and Leonard B. Meyer. *The Rhythmic Structure of Music.*
D'Abreu, Gerald. *Playing the Piano with Confidence.*
Dart, Thurston. *The Interpretation of Music.*
Donington, Robert. *The Interpretation of Early Music.*
Krone, Max. *Expressive Conducting.*
Krueger, Karl. *The Way of the Conductor; His Origins, Purposes, and Procedures.*
Meyer, Leonard B. *Emotion and Meaning in Music.*
Rudolf, Max. *The Grammar of Conducting.*

(Detailed information on these items will be found in the bibliography at the end of the book.)

Content Area 4

THE SCIENCE OF SOUND

The study and presentation of the scientific and mathematical nature of sound should enhance the musical experience of the student both as a performer and as a listener. Among other things, this study should enable him to gain an insight into and an appreciation of the many ways science has extended (and continues to extend) the tonal possibilities available for man to use in making music. Music and science exist too frequently as separate and unrelated entities in the minds of many students. Yet there are understandings to be had from studying science which should lead the student to an improved skill in expressing himself musically. This chapter suggests some of the possibilities inherent in this relationship.

Experiences All Music Classes Should Provide

All students need the opportunity to:

1. Develop an awareness of the varied sounds in their environment, of the diverse industrial, military, and other professional uses of sound, of the ways it is used by other forms of life.

2. Understand the fundamental principles of acoustics through experimentation with musical media, graphic material, and scientific measuring devices. They should know how sound is produced and transmitted. They should understand the role of the sound generator (string, air column, rod, plate, or membrane), transmitting medium (gas, liquid, or solid), receiver (e.g., human ear), and the interpreter (brain). They will understand that the characteristics of a musical sound are determined by the nature of the generator and any resonating cavities, each sound having frequency of vibration, amplitude (or intensity), wave form (or harmonic structure), and duration. Corresponding to the physical characteristic frequency (measured in cycles per second) is the psychological phenomenon known as pitch. Amplitude (measured in decibels) relates to the loudness or softness of the tone and the harmonic structure gives the tone its distinctive quality or timbre. They should also experience the fact that sound can be amplified and transmitted through various mediums, and that musical sound is dependent upon the size, shape, density, and material of the resonating chamber(s) set in motion by sympathetic vibra-

tion. They should also understand that sound can be converted into electrical impulses which can be distorted, transmitted, and/or preserved.

3. Understand the mathematical basis of tonal relationship applied in scale construction, the harmonic series, and key relationships.

4. Understand the mathematical basis of rhythmic relationships.

5. Attain a perspective on the development of musical instruments. This may include:

(a) a comparison of recorded and pictorial examples (and actual performance when available) of the predecessors of present-day instruments;

(b) the development of a "time line" of major changes in the evolution of selected instruments; and

(c) an understanding of how scientific principles are applied in the manufacture of today's instruments.

6. Explore the field of electronic music including (a) efforts to simulate vocal and instrumental sounds electronically, (b) *musique concrete* as used in the entertainment fields for mood and special effects, and (c) of musical composition.

7. Understand, relate, and contrast the hearing process of the human ear with the principles of sound communication as used in broadcasting and recording.

8. Develop understanding of the principles of high fidelity and stereophonic sound. This includes aural and pictorial examples selected from the last eighty-five years of recording.

9. Become aware of and understand the reasons why the acoustical characteristics of school and community facilities differ, and use this understanding in performance and in the selection of seats for concerts.

10. Know some of the musical literature that has been inspired by environmental sounds and phenomena of nature.

Special Experiences for Nonselective Music Classes

In classes which are not primarily performance-oriented, students should have the opportunity to discover and reach conclusions about the acoustics of music through observation, experimentation, field trips, films, reading, and the use of acoustical measuring devices when these are available. If such devices are not available, it is suggested that both teacher and students collect graphic examples from professional literature on this subject. Obviously such a study should involve the science teacher, his laboratory, and its equipment. It is important that students verify their readings through direct experience.

The study of vibration can include seeing and feeling as well as hearing. The nature of vibration in relation to amplification, resonance, and transmission can be demonstrated in the classroom with a minimum of equipment.

Experiments on hearing vibrations.—1. Strike the bass drum and let the sound fade or decay. Strike it again and dampen the head immediately. Compare the difference between the two sounds. "Why did the sound stop?"

2. Grip the clavés tightly in your hands and strike them. Now strike them in the conventional manner. "How and why are the two sounds different?" "Which is the more musical sound?"

Experiments on hearing and feeling vibrations (pitch and resonance in singing).—1. Hold your hand lightly on your throat and sing a low note. "Did your larynx vibrate?" Sing a high note. "What did your larynx do?" "Why?"

2. Hold your hand on your chest and sing a low note. "Do you feel a vibration?" With your hand still on your chest, sing a high note. "Do you feel a vibration in your chest?" "Why not?" Repeat the process with your hand held lightly on your nose. "Why did you feel a vibration in your chest on the low note and in your nasal area on the high note?" "What principle of acoustics have you confirmed?"

3. Sing the following words first in the middle part of your voice, then in a low register, and finally in the high register. Analyze the bodily changes that take place with each different sound in each of the different registers.

"ha, ha, ha"   "hay, hay, hay"

"he, he, he"   "hoo, hoo, hoo"

"ho, ho, ho"

Experiments on sympathetic transmission of vibrations through a solid: amplification.—1. Strike a tuning fork. "How does it move?" Touch it. "How does it feel?"

2. Place an A 440 tuning fork on the piano. Strike A 440 on the piano. "What happens?" "How is the sound transmitted from the piano to the tuning fork?"

3. Place a vibrating tuning fork on an enclosed container (cigar box). "Why does it sound louder?"

Experiments on transmission of vibrations through the air.—1. Place a snare drum near the piano. Strike a chord on the piano. "What happened to the drum?" "Can you see the snare move?"

HARMONIC SERIES

The study of the harmonic series can be a highly involved process for the musically or scientifically unsophisticated student. It is essential that he develop at least minimum understandings with respect to differences in the tone quality of instruments and voices. It is of prime importance that he discover them aurally for himself. The classic experiment included below may need to be demonstrated several times. The use of the many excellent films in this field is a basic part of his experiences. Helpful for some students will be a comparative study of oscillograms of the harmonic spectrums of various instruments and voices sounding the same pitch in different registers. Better still, if an oscillograph is available, a study of the waveforms of different instruments or different voices will vividly demonstrate the existence of differences in the nature of tones produced by the various media.

Experiment. Discover the harmonic series of a music tone and the relative strength of each harmonic.—Press the damper pedal on the piano. Depress but do not sound middle C. Identify C below middle C as the fundamental. Release the damper pedal and strike the fundamental. What pitch sounds? Repeat using other C's and determine which of the C's are the loudest, faintest. Repeat the process using G above middle C and striking the C below middle C.

Present and discuss the harmonic series. Continue the experiment to determine if the students can identify aurally other members of the series and determine which partials or harmonics are the strongest. The second—an octave, the third—a 5th, and the fifth—a 3rd are the most readily distinguished. Students might also be encouraged to:

1. Compare the oscillograms or wave forms of different instruments. (See *Musical Acoustics* by Charles A. Culver, especially Chapter 10, "Stringed Instruments" and Chapter 12, "Wind Instruments" for pictures of wave forms and diagrams of harmonic spectra.)

2. Invite a piano technician to discuss this instrument with the class.

3. Capture the sounds of their town on the tape recorder. Classify those that have identifiable pitch, timbre and intensity; those that are musical and those that are noise.

4. Using a sound-level meter, record the degree of loudness of school sounds such as: talking in a classroom, the record player, students in the corridor, the band playing in its rehearsal room and a single student talking normally in the same room. What is the decibel measurement of each?

5. Experiment with playing percussion instruments in different ways. Compare the sound qualities of each method. Which are the most musical sounds? Use these sounds as instrumental accompaniment to a song. Create percussion ensemble music.

6. Classify the acoustical characteristics of the various rooms, and auditoriums in the school and community. Ex-

plain why some are "dead," others "alive." Does the school chorus sound differently in an empty school auditorium than when the auditorium is full of people? What can be done to improve the acoustical environment of your music room? Experiment with different seating arrangements, reflecting shells, curtains, rugs, and assay differences. Can you explain the presence of an "echo" in a large empty stadium?

7. Listen to recordings and see films of the instrumental music of primitive cultures and other national groups; find pictures of these instruments and compare them with present-day instruments. How do they differ in sight and sound? Explain this difference in terms of acoustical principles.

8. View a movie concerned with instrument making.

9. Prepare for a field trip to a radio or TV station by studying the pictorial diagrams of the manner in which sound waves are converted into electrical energy and transmitted through the air to a radio or TV set.

10. Recreate the Pythagorean experiment with string length to determine pitches used in major scale organization and to establish key relationships. Needed will be a sonometer from the physics laboratory or a replica of the Greek monochord made by a class member.

SCALES AND KEYS

Experiment. Understanding Scale Organization.—Tune the string to a C fork which vibrates at 256 cps. Label this note as the tonic. Divide this string into equal halves. Pluck it; what pitch is sounding? It is C and is vibrating twice as fast. At what frequency? If a tone vibrates at 128 cps, what will it be called? Can a concept or working principle be developed to describe what has happened? *The same name is given to tones when the frequency of one is double the other.*

Allow two-thirds of the string to vibrate. What pitch is sounding? Match it with the piano to determine the answer—G. If its frequency is one and one-half times greater than C, what is its cps?—384. Using the piano, determine the number of white keys from C through G–5. This is why it is called the fifth of the scale and the dominant. Recalling the aural experiment with the harmonic overtone series, why is it given the name dominant?

A key may be defined as a family of tones in which each tone is derived from its subdominant. Using this concept, scales can be completed by determining the frequencies of six tones in addition to the key note. This can be done by multiplying or dividing the frequency of a tone by $1\frac{1}{2}$. Here is a chart of the completed Chain of Dominants for the key of C.

Chain of Dominants

Name	Frequency	Frequency Between 256 and 512
F	171	–––––
C	256	–––––
G	384	–––––
D	576	–––––
A	864	–––––
E	1296	–––––
B	1944	–––––

The next step is to determine the frequencies of the notes with the same letter names between 256 cps and 512 cps. How can this be done mathematically? (Divide or multiply the figure in the middle column by 2 or 4 until a frequency between 256 and 512 results.) Will the application of the first concept work? On completing the final column of the chain of dominants chart F becomes 342; C, 256; G, 384; D, 288; A, 432; E, 324; and B, 486. By arranging the frequencies from the lowest to the highest we have a C major scale.

Project.—Make an 8-stringed instrument based on the C major scale. What frequencies will be used to determine the length of each string? Play some familiar songs on your instrument. How can the violin's strings be of equal length?

Understanding key relationship.—The preceding experiment has demonstrated the ways pitches in a scale can be mathematically determined. The same procedure can be used to establish relationships among keys—the circle of fifths.

Understanding consonance and dissonance.—Harmony also depends on the frequencies of sounds that are heard together. Using the frequencies of the three pitches C 256, E 324, G 384, divide by their common denominator 64. A 4:5:6 relationship results. Students should experiment with notes having this relationship or combinations of small whole numbers 1:2:3:4:5:6:8 to test their consonance.

If one plays middle C 256 on the piano and follows it with C♯ 271, the sound will be dissonant. Why? What is the mathematical relationship of these tones? What are beats? How does the piano tuner use beats?

Students might prepare an historical perspective of recorded sound for presentation to another class, a school assembly, or a community civic club. Such a presentation could include a sequence of dramatized episodes from Thomas A. Edison's historic words "Mary had a little lamb," the recreation of recording sessions in the early 1900's, the middle '30's, through the present with high fidelity and stereophonic sound. It might culminate with a scene of an electronic composer in his laboratory.

Students will have to seek out early recordings and phonographs as well as select the sound recordings most representative of the major advances in recording techniques. They can discover the elementary techniques of sound distortions as used in *musique concrete* by varying the speed of the phonograph. They can learn to recognize distortions used for special effects in the movies, TV, and radio. Through this process they can come to know how man is able to manipulate sound for his own needs and how science has made it possible to preserve music and make it available when needed.

Special Experiences for Instrumental Music Classes

Rehearsals can serve general education purposes if the students are provided with opportunities to:

1. Demonstrate, as needed, some of the suggested acoustical experiments described in the section for *Nonselective Music Classes*.

2. Understand the acoustical principles of the electronic tuner.

3. Apply acoustical principles to the different instruments found in the ensemble, such as: tone generation, transmission, amplification, and resonance.

4. Understand in greater depth the relationship of acoustical principles to the design and construction of their instruments. The class might visit an instrument factory or instrument repair shop. Brass players could demonstrate to the group the purpose of the valves, the relationship between the valves and slide positions of the trombone. Woodwind players might demonstrate the nature of the register key. String players could demonstrate harmonics; bass players show the reason for tuning by harmonics. Publications on acoustics could be examined for charts and pictures of the harmonic spectrum of instruments and their waveforms. A comparison and analyzation should follow.

5. Experiment with wave form as a means of improving tone quality. Invite a fine trumpet player to perform for the oscilloscope. Compare the waveform of certain pitches on a photograph or oscillogram. Allow the trumpet players the time to try to duplicate the picture. After they can do this, ask them to analyze the technical adjustments necessary to do so.[6]

6. Prepare a research paper concerning the evolution and development of an instrument with particular attention

---

[6] Terrence S. Small, "The Use of Oscilloscopic Transparencies as a Diagnostic Tool in the Evaluation of Clarinet Tone Quality." Unpublished dissertation, Western Reserve University, 1964.

given to its design, materials of construction, and the utiliza-
ton of acoustical principles leading to its present design.
Using the "time line," and pictures, make a summary presentation to the class or prepare a bulletin board display.

7. Develop an aural and visual perspective of instrumental timbre through a comparison of the recorded sounds
and pictures of instruments of different periods of music
history.

8. Perform music literature written for the predecessors
of modern instruments. Compare the instrumentation, ex-
tremes of pitch, range, timbre, degree of complexity of the
musical design of the literature with composition which
utilizes the total tonal potential of the modern band or
orchestra. Discuss the question "In what ways has the
application of acoustical principles extended the tonal possibilities of music?"

9. Contrast and characterize the acoustical environments
of the performance and rehearsal situations in the community. Develop the ability to adapt performance to compensate for the unique characteristics of each facility. Involved is the characteristic of reverberation and its control
through absorption, reinforcement, amplification, size, shape,
and height of room. One experience that can well be undertaken in many schools is to determine ways in which the
acoustical environment of the music rehearsal room and
school auditorium can be improved.

10. Understand the effects of temperature and humidity
levels on musical instruments, with implications for musical
performance and care and maintenance of instruments.

Special Experiences for Vocal Music Classes

Students in vocal classes and choral groups should be
provided with the opportunities to:

1. Demonstrate, as needed, some of the suggested acoustical experiments described in the section for *Nonselective
Music Classes.*

2. Understand the fundamental principles of sound generation, vibration, transmission, amplification, and timbre and the function of the various parts of the body involved in singing.

3. Contrast and characterize the acoustical environment of the performance and rehearsal situations in the community. Develop the ability to adapt singing to compensate for the unique characteristics of each facility. Involved is the characteristic of reverberation and its control through absorption, reinforcement, amplification, and the size, shape, and height of rooms.

FILMS

The Nature of Sound

Music As Sound	NET
Music from Mathematics	Bell Tel
Musical Notes	UW
Nature of Sound	Coronet
Science in the Orchestra Series	McGraw-Hill
Hearing the Orchestra, Part I	
Exploring the Instruments, Part II	
Looking at Sounds, Part III	
Science of Sound and Musical Tone	Hammond
Sounds of Music	Coronet
The Synthesis of Music	RCA Victor
Your Voice	EBF

Instruments, Their Historical Development and Manufacture

Begone Dull Care	IFB
Bells of Holland	Films of Nations
Carillon Making	Hoffberg
Development of a Musical Instrument (Harpsichord)	NET
Flute and Harp	NET
Harpsichord	Almanac
Mister B Natural	Conn
Music of India: Instrumental	India
Musical Partnership	NET
New Horizons—Building of a Piano	Baldwin
Primitive Music and Instruments of American Indians	Ambrosch
Rediscovered Harmonies	Film Images
Singing Pipes	NFBC
Sound and the Story	IVT
Story of the Violin	IFB

RECORDINGS

Acoustical Principles

The Science of Sound	Folkways
A Study in High Fidelity	Capitol

Electronic Music

Eight Electronic Pieces	Folkways
Electrogenic Music	Folkways
Panorama of Musique	Ducrett-Thomson
Rhapsodic Variations for Tape Recorder and Orchestra	Louisville
Sounds of New Music	Folkways
Strange to Your Ears	Columbia

Primitive and Ancient Instruments

Baroque Trumpet	Nonesuch
The Birth of the Viol	Bach
Dance Music of Four Centuries	Supraphon
Glass Harmonia Music	Vox
Instruments of the World	Folkways
Italian Lute Music	Harmonia Mundi
Landowska—Art of the Harpsichord	RCA Victor
Man's Early Musical Instruments	Folkways
Music for Harpsichord and Virginal	Folkways
Old Tower Music for Brasses	Cantante
Percussion for Orchestra	Time

Historical Perspective of Recorded Sound

Fifty Years of Grand Opera Singing	RCA Victor
A Musical History of the Boston Symphony Orchestra	RCA Victor

BIBLIOGRAPHY

Instruments

Geiringer, Karl. *Musical Instruments: Their History in Western Culture From the Stone Age to the Present.*
Montgomery, E. R. *The Story Behind Musical Instruments.*
Sachs, Curt. *The History of Musical Instruments.*
Young, Percy M. *Instrumental Music.*

Acoustics

Bartholomew, Wilmer T. *Acoustics of Music.*
Bernade, Arthur. *Horns, Strings, and Harmony.*
Beranek, Leo Leroy. *Music, Acoustics, and Architecture.*
Chavez, Carlos. *Towards New Music.*
Cooper *et al.* "Records by the Billion," *Music in Our Life.*
Cooper *et al.* "The World of Sound in Hi-Fi," *Music in Our Time.*
Culver, Charles. *Musical Acoustics.*

Gelatt, Roland. *The Fabulous Phonograph: From Tin Foil to High Fidelity*.

Helmholtz, Hermann L. F. *On the Sensations of Tone*.

Kinney, Bik. "Experiments in Sound and Music," *Keyboard, Jr.* (October, 1964), p. 4.

Lowrey, H. *A Guide to Musical Acoustics*.

Meyer, Max. *How We Hear: How Tones Make Music*.

North Carolina Department of Public Instruction. "Science of Sound in Music," *Consumer Music for High Schools*.

Read, Oliver, and Walter L. Welch. *From Tin Foil to Stereo: Evolution of the Phonograph*.

Wood, Alexander. *The Physics of Music*.

(Detailed bibliographical information on these items will be found in the bibliography at the end of the book.)

Content Area 5

THE MUSICAL SCORE

Unlike the painter or the sculptor whose works can be observed directly by the viewer, the composer is dependent upon an interpreter—the performer, the conductor, or both —to reveal his work in all its dimensions to the listener. The musical score, in a sense, is the blueprint of the music originating in the mind of the composer. It is the responsibility of the interpreter to reproduce as faithfully as possible the intentions of the composer as outlined in the score.

A musical score will range in complexity from a single line of symbols for an individual voice or instrument to the 20 or more lines required for a contemporary work for large orchestra or a massive work for chorus and orchestra in which there is an individual line of music for each instrument or voice part. While general education objectives cannot be expected to include mastery of the ability to read a complicated score, yet achievement of the modest goals expressed in Outcome IV (see p. 5) will provide the student with a tool that can contribute to his understanding of the art.

It is to be hoped that students will be introduced to musical symbols in the elementary school, as they are to other symbol systems. An understanding of the symbols of musical notation is the key to the musical score but the symbols themselves are meaningless if divorced from their musical context. Work with musical notation should, therefore, always relate directly to musical sounds and never to a mere table of values.

A school should provide access to a library of musical scores. In some instances, sets of scores should be available for student use in class situations. The use of opaque and overhead projectors is recommended as a means of focusing attention on specific passages in a score that requires careful study.

Experiences All Music Classes Should Provide

All students need experiences which will enable them to feel comfortable in the presence of musical notation. The students will:

1. Use musical notation in singing, instrumental, and listening activities. These should be planned to incorporate all elements of the score—the staff, the use of clef signs, pitch indications, rhythmic note values, meter signatures, tempo markings, dynamic markings, and indications of phrasing.

2. Study the development of our system of notation (e.g., the significance of the use of Italian terms; the origin of the clef signs).

3. Follow scores visually while listening to music. In addition, follow a score while listening to phonograph records. This should be understood to also mean encouraging choristers to follow the score of the accompaniment. Orchestra directors might enable certain players (e.g., brass players) to get much more from rehearsals by providing scores for them to follow in passages where their instrument is not employed by the composer. The study of the full score by the whole orchestra (or band) before work on a number begins is psychologically sound.

4. Have experiences of hearing what is seen on a musical score and seeing what is heard (e.g., see the suggested use of "mystery tunes" in Andrews and Leeder, *Guiding Junior-High School Pupils in Music Experiences*, pp. 51-53). A teacher can present the notation (in print or by projector) for a number of musical phrases which the class must match with the sounds as the phrases are played or sung.

Special Experiences for Nonselective Music Classes

Students in those classes in which performance is not the primary activity should engage in special activities in relation to musical notation. Such projects might be to:

1. Experiment with sound to discover the characteristics (duration, pitch, loudness, quality) which must be represented by a symbol system.

2. Devise a means of representing these characteristics not using the staff.

3. Study other cultures to see how they have dealt with this problem.

4. Discuss the question, "What is the relationship between notation and the development of music in Western Civilization?"

5. Examine tablature systems (organ, guitar, ukulele).

6. Learn about the English "tonic sol-fa" system developed by Curwen.

7. Discuss the reasons for the development of shape notes as an "improvement" on the system of staff notation.

Special Experiences for Instrumental Music Classes

Members of school instrumental groups should be encouraged to:

1. Develop an understanding of the transpositions required by certain instruments and of the effect of this on the printed score. The implication here is that all members of an orchestra (or a band) should learn about an orchestra while participating. Students who play non-transposing instruments such as the violin should not be unaware

of the nature of the French horns or clarinets and what this means about the music written for them.

2. Follow the score of the music in rehearsal. The study of the full score by the whole group before work on a composition is recommended. An overhead projector at the conductor's desk can be a valuable teaching tool for this purpose.

3. Study full scores noting the grouping of the instruments on the page and becoming familiar with their names in Italian and German.

4. Develop a vocabulary of musical terms particularly applicable to instrumental music (e.g., *con sordino, arco, pizzicato,* etc.).

5. Compare the arrangement of standard compositions being performed by the school orchestra or band with the original scoring. How do they differ and why?

6. Compare recordings of individual works from the standard instrumental literature. Which interpretation adheres most closely to the composer's intentions as indicated by his score?

7. Compare settings of a composition for both band and orchestra. William Schuman has scored "Chester" for both band and orchestra and recordings of both versions are available. Sousa's march, *The Stars and Stripes Forever,* is also available in recordings by both band and orchestra.

8. Listen, with score in view, to instrumental selections representative of various musical styles and periods. The following brief list contains suggestions of works which might be used for this purpose and which have been recorded. Many of them might also be performed by school musicians.

ENSEMBLES

Bach	Suites 2 and 3
Barber	Summer Music (for woodwind quintet)
Beethoven	Quartets, Op. 18, Nos. 3 and 4
Bruch, M.	Eight Trios, Op. 38 (clarinet, viola or cello and piano)
Dahl, I.	Allegro and Arioso (woodwind quintet)
Gabrieli	Canzon septimi toni (brass chorus)

Glinka, M.	Trio Pathetique (clarinet, bassoon, piano)
Haydn	Divertimento in E
Hindemith	Kleine Kammermusik, Op. 24, No. 2
Hovhaness	Suite, Op. 99 (violin, piano, percussion)
Milhaud	The Chimney of King René (woodwind) quintet)
Mozart	Serenade in c minor, K.388 (oboes, clarinets, horns, bassoons, 7 each)
Mozart	Clarinet Quintet, K.581
Persichetti	The Hollow Men (trumpet and strings)
Pezel, J.	Sonatas 2 and 22 (brass quintet)
Prokofiev	Quintet, Op. 39 (oboe, clarinet, violin, viola, string bass)
Purcell, H.	Music for Queen Mary II (brass quartet)
Ravel	Quartet in F Major
Schubert	"Trout" Quintet

ORCHESTRA

Bach	Brandenburg Concertos
Beethoven	Symphony No. 1
Brahms	Academic Festival Overture
Chabrier	Espana
Copland	El Salon Mexico
Corelli	Concerto Grosso, Op. 6, No. 8 (strings)
Debussy	Nocturnes
Dvořák	New World Symphony
Fine, I.	Diversions for Orchestra
Haydn	Symphony No. 101 (The Clock)
Kodály	Intermezzo (from *Háry János*)
McBride, R.	Pumpkin Eater's Little Fugue (strings)
Mendelssohn	Fingal's Cave Overture
Mozart	*Idomeneo* Overture
Mussorgsky	A Night on Bald Mountain
Riegger	Dance Rhythms
Vivaldi	Concerto in d minor, Op. 3, No. 11 (strings)
Wagner	*Die Meistersinger* Overture
Weber	Overture to *Oberon*

BAND

Bergsma	March with Trumpets
Bruckner	Apollo March
Gossec	Classic Overture
Grainger	Children's March "Over the Hills and Far Away"
Holst	First Suite in E Flat
Mendelssohn	Military Overture in C
Milhaud	Suite Française

Schuman	Chester Overture from *New England Triptych*
Sousa	El Capitan
Strauss, R.	Serenade in Eb Major
Stravinsky	Symphonies for Wind Instruments
Vaughan Williams	Folk Song Suite
Wagner	Trauersinfonie

Special Experiences for Vocal Music Classes

Students in vocal classes and performing groups should have the opportunity to:

1. Develop, through study and practice, sufficient skill in reading music to carry a vocal part independently. This should be a major objective of any elective vocal music offering, and progress should be evaluated at regular intervals. Independence will be encouraged through considerable experience in small ensembles. Quartets and octets within the choirs are recommended.

2. Become aware of the significance and importance of the various vocal parts of the compositions being sung. Attention should be paid to the way in which they are notated (e.g., the use of the bass clef).

3. Compare recordings of individual works from the standard choral literature. Which interpretation adheres most closely to the composer's intentions as indicated by his score?

4. Develop a vocabulary of musical terms particularly applicable to vocal music (e.g., *sotto voce, mit gänzlich, gedampfter Stimme, parlanté,* etc.).

5. Compare arrangements of familiar songs for mixed chorus and male chorus. What has the arranger done to the original setting? Why?

6. Study vocal scores of operas or oratorios. What is the principle by which the voice parts are arranged on the page? How can you tell which staff is for the chorus and which for the soloist?

7. Listen, with score in view, to representative choral selections of varying styles and periods including both *a cappella* works and selections with orchestral accompaniment. The following list suggests some works that might

be used for this purpose and which have been recorded. Many of them might also be performed by school groups in whole or in part.

ENSEMBLES

Brahms	Liebeslieder Waltzes	Associated
Donizetti	Sextet from *Lucia*	G. Schirmer
Hindemith	Since All Is Passing	Associated
Lassus	O Eyes of My Beloved	E. C. Schirmer
Morley	Now Is the Month of Maying	Gray
Purcell	Choruses from *Dido and Aeneas*	Oxford
Verdi	Quartet from *Rigoletto*	G. Schirmer
Wilbye	Adieu, Sweet Amaryllis	Presser

CHORUSES

Bach	*Magnificat*	Gray
Bloch	Sacred Service	Broude
Brahms	*German Requiem*	G. Schirmer
Britten	*A Ceremony of Carols*	Boosey & Hawkes
English Madrigals		
Handel	*Messiah*	G. Schirmer
Hanson	Song of Democracy	C. Fischer
Mozart	Ave Verum Corpus	G. Schirmer
Palestrina	Sicut Cervus	G. Schirmer
Prokofiev	*Alexander Nevsky*	Leeds
Purcell	O Sing Unto The Lord	E. C. Schirmer
Schubert	*Mass in G*	G. Schirmer
Thompson	Alleluia	E. C. Schirmer
Verdi	*Requiem*	G. Schirmer
Victoria	O Magnum Mysterium	G. Schirmer
Vivaldi	*Gloria*	Colombo
Walton	*Belshazzar's Feast*	Oxford

FILMS

An A B C for Music	Pictura
The Alphabet in Black	NET
The Alphabet in White	NET
Aural Memory	NET
Beethoven: Eroica and Pastoral	NET
The Classical Achievement	NET
The Classical Orchestra	NET
Conducting Good Music	EBF
The Elements of Composition	NET
Essay in Sound	NET
Forms of Music—Instrumental	Coronet
The Grand Plan	NET
Harmony in Music	Coronet
How We Write Music	Iowa State

Key Feeling	NET
Meter and Rhythm	NET
The Orchestra Expanded	NET
Schubert and Mendelssohn	NET
The String Trio	Coronet
Time in Music	NET
Tonalities Old and New	NET

BIBLIOGRAPHY

Bernstein, Martin. *Score Reading.*

Bockman, Guy Alan, and William J. Starr. *Scored for Listening.*

Fiske, Roger. *Score Reading.* Book I, Orchestration; Book II, Musical Form; Book III, Concertos.

Starr, William J., and George F. Devine. *Music Scores Omnibus.* Parts I and II.

(Detailed bibliographical information for these items will be found in the bibliography at the end of the book.)

Content Area 6

HISTORICAL CONSIDERATIONS

There are historical implications underlying all music instruction in the classroom and the rehearsal. The function of the structural and expressive elements of music should not be studied apart from their historical or stylistic context, for the evolution of these elements constitutes a major ingredient in the history of music. In turn these elements will be better understood if placed in historical perspective. Additional to these understandings are those related to music and society, to music and art, and to the composer and his music.

It is not likely, or perhaps even desirable, that the study of music will often be from a purely historical approach. Broad understandings rather than quantities of information should be the objective; nevertheless large concepts and relationships have to be substantiated by content and related directly to musical experiences. Understandings related to composers, styles, and analyses all bear upon one another and certainly grow out of the use and knowledge of music itself. In planning the curriculum for music in general education some consideration must be given to the point in history where the study should begin, the proportion of attention given to various music periods or to related cultural and historical developments, and to how much of the world should be encompassed (American, Oriental, Latin-American, or mainly European). All music teachers, whether they deal primarily with performance groups or other classes, should then make appropriate contributions in their teaching to this agreed-upon minimum. Great care must be taken in planning the over-all curriculum in order that there will be provision for each student to integrate his learning about music history.

Experiences All Music Classes Should Provide

In order that they may develop historical perspective in connection with their musical experiences, all students should be provided with opportunities to:

1. Relate musical compositions studied to political or intellectual movements of the time (e.g., Beethoven and the French Revolution, Monteverdi and the change from madrigal composition to works for the stage, Stravinsky and his impact on the 20th century).

2. Enlarge their musical vocabulary and improve their pronunciation of foreign words and phrases.

3. Develop their ability to use the library, program notes, and criticisms in relating their musical experiences to their knowledge of history.

4. Compare the ways in which composers throughout history have treated the basic elements of their art and how they have employed the principles of rhythm, color, unity, contrast, and balance.

5. Become aware of man's constant search for new and expanded means for creating musical sound through study of the history of musical instruments.

6. Acquire the broad picture of the major periods in music history and become familiar with the major forms, stylistic characteristics, and major composers of each period.

7. Develop an understanding of the place and use of music in society at a certain time in history and of how music provides another insight into the spirit of the period.

Special Experiences for Nonselective Music Classes

Students in classes where performance of music is not a major activity should have the opportunity to become familiar with music of all ages. Though this exposure does not need to be chronological, or even primarily historically oriented, the experiences should be broad enough to assure the development of historical perspective. To this end students might be encouraged to:

1. Examine how Pythagoras constructed the scale, observing the change in expressive quality with the movement of the half step. Compare with our major and minor scales.

2. Sing monophonic music of the Middle Ages, comparing the line, rhythm, phrasing, and expressiveness of chant with other forms of unisonal melody.

3. Sing songs in organum style, songs of the Crusaders and troubadours, rounds and canons. (See Robbins, *Early English Christmas Carols*, or Greenberg, *An English Song Book*.)

4. Imitate a medieval instrumental accompaniment with drum and recorder.

5. Study the use of music in the "mysteries" and "miracle plays" (e.g., "Lully Lulla," the carol from the pageant of the Shearmen and Tailor's Company at Coventry). Listen to Noah Greenberg's recording of the *Play of Daniel*.

6. Trace the development of staff notation.

7. Examine the products of the visual arts in the Romanesque and Gothic periods and draw relationships to musical characteristics.

8. Compare 13th century and 16th century examples of choral music. What voices sing in each? Which sounds more "modern" and why? (e.g., Motet, "Aucun" of Petrus

de Cruce, *Historical Anthology of Music*, Vol. I, No. 34, and Motet "Tristis est anima mea" of Orlandus Lassus in *Masterpieces of Music Before 1750.*)

9. Describe what is meant by "a cappella" singing; listen to examples of choral polyphony as exemplified by Palestrina, Victoria, or Byrd.

10. Sing melodies of chorales which students can find in their hymnals at church. Compare the texture of chorales with polyphony. Discuss the source of the chorale melodies, their use in services, the influence of the printing of music.

11. Contrast the spirit and texture of Renaissance sacred music with examples of secular music of the period (e.g., madrigals by Morley or Gesualdo).

12. Sing English madrigals and discuss their popularity in Elizabethan England.

13. Relate the development of opera, oratorio, cantata, solo song, suite, concerto, and sonata to the "spirit of the age" of the 17th century.

14. Make a list of Baroque composers whose works are performed in their community and on radio and television during the month. Discuss their importance to music.

15. Compare the style of a Handel oratorio with that of Haydn.

16. Do the research and prepare the program notes for a presentation of the "Classic period" by the school orchestra and chorus.

17. Compare the events in the lives of George Washington and F. Joseph Haydn, both born in 1732.

18. View the film "The Magnificent Rebel" based on the life of Beethoven.

19. Search for evidences of change in keyboard music occasioned by the invention of the pianoforte.

20. Diagram the growth in the instrumentation of the symphony orchestra during the 19th century.

21. Debate the topic "Richard Wagner has had more influence on musical theatre than Claudio Monteverdi."

22. Make lists of distinguishing characteristics that will help a listener identify compositions from Baroque, Classic, Romantic, Impressionistic, and Contemporary periods of music history.

23. Listen to electronic music and discuss its relevance to our times.

24. Make a time chart of 100 important composers who lived between 1200 and 1965.

Special Experiences for Instrumental Music Classes

Students of instrumental music need to develop an historical perspective to make their performing experiences more meaningful. To this end they might be given the opportunity to:

1. Look up the kinds and functions of early instruments. Compare them with their modern counterparts.

2. Perform and listen to works based on ancient subjects (e.g., Beethoven's *Prometheus*).

3. Compare early tablature notation with present day musical notation.

4. Select certain instrumentalists and singers to illustrate voice-instrument fusion in medieval music.

5. Contrast instrumental and vocal style.

6. Illustrate modern use of elaboration, embellishment, improvisation, imitation, and variation.

7. Describe tone quality, construction, playing style of lute, viol, and early keyboard instruments.

8. Play Renaissance dance forms. Suggest suitable "pairs" of modern dance forms.

9. Learn to play the recorder; form a recorder consort. Look up what other Renaissance "combos" there were. Join with singers to present a Renaissance program for choir, band, other music classes.

10. Play music selected to build a complete curriculum in which would be studied (a) major composers, (b) stylistic characteristics, (c) structural means, (d) development of instrumentation and refinement of tone quality, (e) repre-

sentative forms, and (f) interpretive principles of the Baroque, Classic, Romantic, and Contemporary periods.

11. Perform as soloists and ensemble members to illustrate for other music classes or for the school assembly.

12. Prepare as part of a concert or festival presentation a topic or composition with proper comment, analysis, illustration. Rehearse the organization, timing, and presentation as well as the playing, and then perform the entire offering.

13. Build a harpsichord and other early instruments from kits and then learn to use them in class and concert performances.

Special Experiences for Vocal Music Classes

Students of choral music will better understand the music they sing if they can relate it to its place in musical history. To enable them to do this, they might be given the opportunity to:

1. Learn about the nature and function of the Greek chorus and the soloist in early drama; work with drama and dance departments in performing excerpts; listen to later works on Greek themes (e.g., Stravinsky's *Oedipus Rex*).

2. Listen to and analyze tone quality and style of chant singing. Study modal and syllabic structure of chants.

3. Sing examples of "ars antiqua" and "ars nova" and observe development of part singing and choral style (e.g., *Motet* of the School of Notre Dame, *Conductus*, *Agnus Dei* of Machaut, and *Ballata* by Landini—Numbers 10, 11, 13, and 14 in *Masterpieces of Music Before 1750*).

4. Compare medieval and modern notation; look up ecclesiastical derivation of nomenclature and symbols. Study Latin text pronunciation.

5. Sing a 14th and also a 16th century motet and describe the expressive differences and the musical means used. (See motets of Machaut, Gombert, Palestrina, Lassus, and Byrd in *Historical Anthology of Music*, Vol. I.)

6. Experience first hand the music of Des Pres, Lassus, Palestrina, to know what is meant by Renaissance vocal polyphony being considered as one of history's high points of musical beauty.

7. Prepare a presentation by a small group (a quarter of the class in each group) for the class on one of the following: Netherlands, Roman, Venetian, and Reformation styles.

8. Study the development of the Mass; sing and listen to outstanding examples; hear a cathedral performance.

9. Discuss the social use and musical style of the madrigal. Soloists and small groups might perform chansons and lute songs for the choir, other music classes, or assembly.

10. Sing music selected to build a complete curriculum in which would be studied (a) major composers, (b) stylistic characteristics, (c) structural means, (d) treatment of the voices, (e) representative forms, and (f) interpretive principles of the Baroque, Classic, Romantic, and Contemporary periods.

11. Prepare, as part of a concert or festival presentation, a composition or a unified series of numbers with proper comment, analysis, and illustrations. Rehearse the organization, timing, and presentation as well as the singing and then perform the entire offering.

12. Join forces with instrumental groups to present oratorios or dramatic works of historical significance, (e.g., Rousseau's *Le Devin du Village*).

STRING ORCHESTRA

Easy

Aker	Little Classic Suite	C. Fischer
Brahms	Waltz	G. Schirmer
Byrd-Collins	Pavan	Fox
Grieg-Maddy	Im Balladenton	Remick
Handel	Bourree	Remick
Haydn-Lotzenhiser	Minuet	C. Fischer
McKay	Sea Spray Suite	Elkan-Vogel
Mozart	Minuetto from *Don Juan*	Remick

Medium

Bach-Schenkman	Choral Prelude, "Come Now, Thou Saviour"	Galaxy

Bartók-Willner	Roumanian Folk Dances	Boosey & Hawkes
Beethoven-Woodhouse	Rondo Expressivo	Boosey & Hawkes
Cowell	Hymn and Fuguing Tune No. 2	Associated
Frescobaldi-Elkan	Suite in D	Elkan-Vogel
Gesualdo-Kramer	Madrigal	G. Schirmer
Haydn-Palmer-Best	A Haydn Suite	Oxford
Mendelssohn-Watson	Praeludium, Op. 7, No. 2	Witmark
Mozart-Woodhouse	Three Divertimento Movements	Boosey & Hawkes
Schubert-Maro	Three Little Pieces	Boosey & Hawkes
White	Prelude and Ostinato	G. Schirmer

Difficult

Arensky	Variations on a Theme by Tchaikovsky	Broude
Bach-Glass	Organ Concerto in a minor	Associated
Bach-Whittaker	Sinfonias from *Cantatas 12, 21, or 106*	Oxford
Cadman	American Suite	Henri Elkan
Corelli	Concerto Grosso, Op. 6, No. 8	Kalmus
Hindemith	Five Pieces	Associated
Mozart	Serenade in Four Movements	C. Fischer
Sibelius	Rakastava (the Lover)	So.Mus.Pub. Co.
Vivaldi	Concerto Grosso in d minor	Oxford
Walton	Crown Imperial	Oxford

ORCHESTRA

Easy

Bach-Walter	Jesu, Joy of Man's Desiring	Berkeley
Bartók	Five Pieces for Younger Orchestras	Remick
Beethoven-Benoy	Hymn of Joy	Oxford
Bizet-Seredy	*Carmen* Selection	C. Fischer
Gluck-Mottl	Petit Suite de Ballet	C. Fischer
Handel-Woodhouse	March from *Scipio*	Boosey & Hawkes
Haydn-Isaac	Andante from *Surprise Symphony*	C. Fischer
Mendelssohn-Roberts	Cornelius Festival March	C. Fischer

Mozart-Jurey	Cavatina and Air	Carlin
Purcell-Gardner	Trumpet Voluntary	Staff
Scarlatti-Filas	Aria and Minuet	Pro Art

Medium

Beethoven	Ruins of Athens	Broude
Copland	Waltz from *Billy the Kid*	Boosey & Hawkes
Debussy-Isaac	Reverie	Belwin
Dvořák-Stone	Slavonic Dance, Op. 46, No. 8	Boosey & Hawkes
Gounod-Isaac	Music from *Faust*	Belwin
Haydn-Winter	Symphony No. 7 in C Major	Boosey & Hawkes
Lully-Murphy	French Baroque Suite	Witmark
Mozart	*Cosi Fan Tutte*, Overture	C. Fischer
Schubert-Weaver	*Rosamunde*, Overture	Mills
Van Hoesen-Hunt	Living Music from the Past	C. Fischer
Verrall	Symphony for Young Orchestras	Boston
Vivaldi-Muller	Vivaldi Violin Concerto	Robbins

Difficult

Bach-Stokowski	Fugue in g minor (The Shorter)	Broude
Beethoven	Symphony No. 6 (Pastorale)	Kalmus
Chabrier	España	Kalmus
Couperin-Milhaud	Overture and Allegro from *La Sultana*	Elkan-Vogel
Kodály	Intermezzo from *Háry János*	Boosey & Hawkes
Mozart	Symphony No. 40 in g minor	C. Fischer
Prokofiev	Classical Symphony	Kalmus
Sibelius	Karelia Suite, Op. 11	G. Schirmer
Wagner	*Die Meistersinger* (Overture)	C. Fischer, Kalmus

BAND

Easy

Bach-Lake	Sixteen Chorales	G. Schirmer
Beethoven-Gordon	German Dance	Mills
Chopin-Tolmage	Two Chopin Preludes, No. 4 and No. 20	Staff
Handel-Ford	Baroque Suite	Pro Art
Humperdinck-Erickson	Hansel and Gretel	Belwin

| Mozart-Tolmage | Minuetto, *Symphony No. 39 in E Flat* | Staff |
| Ravel-Johnson | Pavanne | Rubank |

Medium

Bach-Moehlmann	Prelude and Fugue in f minor	FitzSimons
Bartók-Suchoff	Four Pieces for Band	Fox
Frescobaldi-Slocum	Toccata	Mills
Gossec	Military Symphony in F	Mercury
Handel-Kay	*Water Music* Suite	Presser
Mozart-Barnes	*The Impresario*, Overture	Ludwig
Offenbach-Isaac	Ballet Parisienne	C. Fischer
Saint-Saëns-Elkus	Prelude and Processional	Marks
Strauss-Beeler	*Gypsy Baron* Suite	G. Schirmer

Difficult

Bach-Goldman	In Dulci Jubilo	G. Schirmer
Copland	An Outdoor Overture	Boosey & Hawkes
Fauchet-Gillette	*Symphony in B Flat*, Movement I or IV	Witmark
Giannini	Praeludium and Allegro	Colombo
Holst	Suite No. 1 in E Flat	Boosey & Hawkes
Mennin	Canzona	C. Fischer
Mozart-Krance	Overture to *Titus*	Witmark
Persichetti	Divertimento for Band	Presser

CHORAL-SATB

Easy

Bach-Hirt	Alleluia! Sing Praise	C. Fischer
Franck-Heller	Panis Angelicus	SHM
Franz	Dedication	Summy-Birchard
Hassler-Greyson	My Heart with Love Is Springing	Bourne
Mozart-Craig	Invocation	Plymouth
Palestrina-Schroth	O God We Worship Thee	Kjos
Ringwald	The Four Freedoms	Shawnee
Scheidt	O Saviour Sweet	Marks
Schubert	Sanctus	Staff
Sweelinck	We Have Heard the Words	Marks

Tkach, arr.	We Praise Thee	Kjos
Zhadanov	We Praise Thee	Boosey & Hawkes

Medium

Bach-Klein	Glory and Honor	SHM
Des Pres-Merrill	The Cricket	Oxford
di Lasso-Hirt	I Know A Young Maiden	C. Fischer
Franck	Psalm 150	C. Fischer
Gibbons	Almighty and Everlasting God	Bourne
Mendelssohn	Not Only Unto Him	Belwin
Morley	Now Is the Month of Maying	Gray
Mozart-Ehret	Lacrymosa	Pro Art
Palestrina-Gerhard	Adoramus Te	Spratt
Schubert	To Music	Gillman
Schuetky-Scott	Send Forth Thy Spirit	Hoffman
Schumann-Jenkins	I'll Not Lament	SHM
Siegmeister, arr.	On My Journey Home	Presser
Tcherepnin	Tranquil Light	Boosey & Hawkes
Thomson	My Shepherd Will Supply My Need	Gray
Vaughan Williams-Rosenberg	Sine Nomine (For All the Saints)	C. Fischer

Difficult

Bach-Ehret	Gloria in Excelsis Deo	Boosey & Hawkes
Brahms-Field	Blessed They	Boosey & Hawkes
Brahms-Jenkins	We Wandered	SHM
Carissimi	Plorate Filii Israel	Bourne
di Lasso	Echo Song	Flammer, Kjos E. C. Schirmer G. Schirmer
Fauré	Cantique de Jean Racine	Broude
Gibbons-Greyson	The Silver Swan	Bourne
Handel-Wagner	Mourn, All Ye Muses	Lawson-Gould
Haydn	Sing With Joy and Gladness	Marks
Hovhaness	Alleluia	Peters
Ives	Sixty-Seventh Psalm	Associated
Kodály	Psalm 114	Boosey & Hawkes

Mozart	Sanctus and Hosanna	Boosey & Hawkes
Schein	Who With Grieving Soweth	Mercury
Sweelinck	Hodie Christus Natus Est	Colombo

RECORDINGS

Archive Research Periods I-XII	Archive
History of Music in Sound	RCA
Masterpieces of Music Before 1750	Haydn Society
Music Appreciation Records	Book of the Month Club
2,000 Years of Music	Folkways

BIBLIOGRAPHY

Apel, Willi. *Harvard Dictionary of Music.*

Baker's Biographical Dictionary of Musicians.

Baldwin, Lillian. *A Listener's Anthology of Music.* Volume I, "The Master Builders;" Volume II, "The Musician As Poet, Painter, and Dramatist."

Bauer, Marion, and Ethel Peyser. *How Music Grew.*

Berger, Melvin. *Choral Music in Perspective.*

Collins, Walter S. "A selected list of Renaissance and Baroque choral works with sacred English texts in practical editions."

Coover, James, and Richard Colvig. *Medieval and Renaissance Music on Long-Playing Records.*

Cotton, Edith M. *Historical Panorama.* Student's Chart, 17" x 22".

Davison, Archibald T. *Historical Anthology of Music.* Vols. I and II.

Ernst, Karl, *et al. Birchard Music Series.* Books 7 and 8.

Greenberg, Noah. "A selective list of XV and XVI century Netherlandish choral music available in practical editions."

Greenberg, Noah. *The English Song Book.*

Grout, Donald J. *A History of Western Music.*

Hartshorn, William C., and Helen S. Leavitt. *Making Friends with Music.*

Hickok, Robert. "A selective list of Baroque choral works in practical editions."

Keyboard Junior Magazine.

La Rue, Jan, and John Vinton. "A selective list of choral compositions from the classical period in practical editions."

Let's Explore Music Series.

Lippman, Edward A. *Musical Thought in Ancient Greece.*

McGehee, Thomasine. *People and Music.*

Opera News.

Parrish, Carl, and John F. Ohl. *Masterpieces of Music Before 1750.*

Pincherle, Marc. *An Illustrated History of Music.*

Portnoy, Julius. *Music in the Life of Man.*

Rafferty, Sadie, and Nick Rossi. *Music Through the Centuries.*

Record Hunter, The. *Institutional Order Book for Long-Playing Records.*
Richardson, Allen L., and Mary E. English. *Living with Music.*
Robbins, Rossell Hope. *Early English Christmas Carols.*
Serposs, Emile, and Ira Singleton. *Music in Our Heritage.*
Shetler, Donald J. *Film Guide for Music Educators.*
Starr, William J., and George F. Devine. *Music Scores Omnibus.* Parts I and II.
Ulrich, Homer, and Paul A. Pisk. *A History of Music and Musical Style.*

(Detailed bibliographical information on these items will be found in the bibliography at the end of the book.)

Content Area 7

MUSIC AND MAN

Man is a spiritual, aesthetic, rational, social, and skillful being. In each of these fundamental traits man has found music to be a means of expression. By fashioning tonal-rhythmic arrangements, man in every age and every culture has found a satisfying way to help him communicate better with his God, satisfy his aesthetic impulses, relieve his labors, express his feelings about himself, his fellow man, and his world. This section concerns itself with some of the ways the student may look into the many uses of music by man.

Experiences All Music Classes Should Provide

In the course of their school experience, students should have the opportunity to:

1. Explore the numerous ways in which music is a part of their own living and of the life of their community. (See Content Area 11.)

2. Develop an insight into the association between music and man's spiritual nature and values; develop a sensitivity to music's transcendent expressiveness.

3. Become aware of music's close connection with the numerous social activities of man at different periods of history.

4. Gain knowledge of music's use in medicine and therapy in early and contemporary times; analyze music's effect upon one's varied emotional states or sense of well-being.

5. Develop an awareness of society's influence on taste.

6. Discuss the necessity of aesthetic education in the schools.

Special Experiences for Nonselective Music Classes

In classes which are not primarily performance oriented, students might be encouraged to explore in some depth man's many relationships with music. Such classes should seek ways of sharing their findings with the rest of the school.

MUSIC AND RELIGION

In examining the relationship between music and religion, classes might:

1. Study how primitive man, past and present, has used music in religious rites. Invite an anthropologist to talk to the class. Listen to and study the story of Stravinsky's *Rite of Spring*. Try to find recordings of genuine primitive religious music.

2. Discover the stories illustrating the ancients' belief in the supernatural creation of music. Search for music based on these tales (e.g., Apollo, Orpheus, Pan, the Muses, Jubal, Huang Ti). See Bulfinch, *Mythology of Greece and Rome;* Portnoy, *Music in the Life of Man;* Genesis 4:21; and "Chinese Music," *Encyclopaedia Britannica*.

3. Listen to, play, and sing early chants, hymns, chorales to sense their spirituality. Try to discover how these songs are "of the folk" and how they have been used to strengthen and teach a people. Try to explain why some peoples have banned music; e.g., See Elizabeth May, "The Influence of the Meiji Period on Japanese Children's Music," *Journal of Research in Music Education*, XIII (Summer, 1965).

4. Compare genuine hymns and spirituals with commercial religious tunes and texts.

MUSIC AND SOCIAL MAN

To understand the social nature of music, classes might:

1. List ten different practical or social uses of music.

2. Examine the differences between sacred and secular music. Look up the history of the tune *Greensleeves* in Eric Routley's *The English Carol* and *The Hymnal 1940 Companion*. Where did Luther get his chorale melodies?

3. Determine different functional uses of folk songs. Listen to both a genuine folk song and a commercial song of a similar nature; try to discover wherein the difference lies. How does an Irish folk song differ from a German one; a Scotch song from a Mexican; a Chinese song from an Israeli one?

4. Attempt to discover why folk songs and folk singing enjoy their present popularity. What is taking the place of song during work for today's industrial worker?

5. Discuss such questions as "Can music that is only for entertainment be degrading as the ancients believed? Are some kinds of music less desirable than other kinds? What happens to man, music, and society if entertainment sinks too low, if taste becomes too indiscriminating?"

6. Study, sing, and play the music of the Troubadours. What do you know about the kinds of music man used for pleasure at different times in history? (See Content Area 6.)

MUSIC AND THERAPY

An interest in music and therapy might be developed if classes were to:

1. Make observations of doctors' and dentists' use of music.

2. Look up Biblical and Greek references to the use of music to soothe and heal. What effects do different kinds of music have on you when you are ill? (See I Samuel 16:23; Homer's *Odyssey*.)

3. Investigate music's use in psychotherapy.

MUSIC AND VALUES

Some classes, particularly of older students, may benefit from study designed to:

1. Determine if, in our own society, there are kinds of music which might be considered degrading? Will imitation of the undesirable qualities of this music result from participation in it? Has society's view of jazz changed in the past fifty years? Does today's "Jazz Mass" elevate the human spirit?

2. Decide whether or not man takes on bravery from military music, goodness from gentle music, coarseness from noisy music.

3. Assign different emotional states to our major and minor modes. Listen to the several Greek modes to see if the expressive quality the Greeks ascribed to each mode can be detected.

4. Determine (a) the Greeks' attitude toward changes in the modes and (b) the history of innovation in music throughout the centuries. (See Plato's *Republic*.)

5. Develop familiarity with the Greek concept that music should be controlled by the state for the good of the state. Does any contemporary country share this belief, and, if so, how does it enforce musical censorship? (See Solon, Damon, and Plato.)

OTHER CONSIDERATIONS

Students might be encouraged to think about music in new ways by seeking answers to questions such as the following:

1. In addition to the functional uses to which music may be put, such as liturgical or military, what other uses are made of it?

2. If we took away man's creative and aesthetic characteristics, what kind of a man would remain? What are the implications for the world's future? For education?

3. What arts have developed from the senses of man? How have music and the fine arts imitated and idealized

nature? What is the difference between "sound effects" music and music which suggests the sounds of nature, such as Debussy's *La Mer?*

4. Are your feelings better expressed in some types of music than others? What emotions can you find expressed in musical compositions? (See "The Capurso Study" in *Music and Your Emotions.*)

5. Do you think you can obtain a better understanding of what men were like in earlier times by listening to or playing and singing music from various historical periods?

6. What should you, your school, and community, do to allow you to develop your aesthetic sensitivities?

Special Experiences for Instrumental Music Classes

Students of instrumental music may gain a better idea of the role of music in the life of men if they are encouraged to:

1. Trace historically the use of their instruments, or their predecessors, in religious ceremonies, for social or recreational purposes. Students should share their findings with others in the group or possibly with the school through the preparation of an assembly program.

2. Examine how music creates religious mood and meaning as they prepare sacred works for performance. What elements of performance produce the desired effects?

3. Seek ways in which they can use their musical skills in their own church services.

4. Determine the original function of the music they perform in concert: What was the social milieu of its creation? (e.g., A brass choir might compare the circumstances which produced the Josquin *Royal Fanfare,* Gabrieli's *Sonata pian'e forte,* a Pezel *Sonata,* and Henry Cowell's *Fanfare for Forces of Latin American Allies.*)

5. Compare a commercial recording of a folk song with the same song arranged for a school instrumental group and attempt to discover wherein the difference lies.

6. Compare the unique characteristics of the folk music of various countries. (e.g., An orchestra might prepare a

program for other music classes using Brahms' *Hungarian Dances,* Dvořák's *Slavonic Dances,* Grainger's *Molly on the Shore,* McKay's *Scenes from the Southwest,* Mussorgsky's *Cossack Dance,* Swinach's *Danza Andaluza.*)

7. Evaluate how music has been an aesthetic influence in their own lives. How can tastes be further refined?

8. Evaluate the cultural influence of the instrumental program in the school and community. Student suggestions for expanding or improving this influence should be sought.

9. Study the opportunities to play their instruments in the community after graduation. Comparisons might be made with other communities of similar size and make-up in preparation for planning more opportunities.

Special Experiences for Vocal Music Classes

Students of vocal music may gain a better understanding of the role of music in the life of man if they are encouraged to:

1. Search for the spiritual message in the sacred music they perform. Students should try to determine how the music communicates its message, what meanings remain constant in compositions from different centuries, and what changes in the musical language occur.

2. Identify the churches and synagogues in the community which feature fine vocal music and attend services.

3. Trace the role of singing in man's social and recreational activities throughout history.

4. Determine the reason for the composition of the works they perform in concert. What was the social milieu of the music's creation? (e.g., A vocal ensemble compares the circumstances which produced Bach's *Jesu, Priceless Treasure;* Hassler's *Dancing and Springing;* Hindemith's *Since All Is Passing;* Morley's *Now Is the Month of Maying;* Mozart's *Ave Verum;* Purcell's *In These Delightful Pleasant Groves;* Ravenscroft's *New Oysters;* Sullivan's *Sing a Merry Madrigal; Sumer Is Icumen In;* and Vaughan Williams' *O Taste and See.*)

5. Seek ways in which they can use their musical talents in their own church services or in serving other community agencies.

6. Compare the unique characteristics of the folk music of various countries. What does the music suggest about the people who created it?

7. Compare genuine folk expression as gathered by a folklorist with choral arrangements used in class, and with commercialized "folk music."

8. Evaluate how music has been an aesthetic influence in their own lives. How can tastes be further refined?

9. Evaluate the cultural influence of the choral program in the school and community. Students' suggestions for expanding or improving this influence should be sought.

10. Study the opportunities to continue singing after leaving school. Comparisons might be made with other communities of similar size and make-up in preparation for planning more or different opportunities.

STRING ORCHESTRA

Easy

Bach	March in D	Remick
Handel	Bourree	Remick
Holesovsky	Variations on a French Folk Tune	Henri Elkan
Sontag	Folk Song Set	Galaxy

Medium

Bach-Bantock	Sheep May Safely Graze	Mills
Bornschein, arr.	Four Russian Numbers	Presser
Cowell	Hymn and Fuguing Tune No. 2	Associated
Fellowes	Eight Short Elizabethan Dance Tunes	Galaxy
Grieg	Norwegian Melody (Folio)	G. Schirmer
Handel-Baines	Suite from *Water Music*	Oxford
McKay, arr.	Three Folk Songs	Presser
Purcell-Bridgewater	Ayres for the Theatre	Mills
Schubert-Dubensky	Round Dance	Colombo

Difficult

Bach	Brandenburg Concerto No. 3	Boosey & Hawkes

Bach-Casadesus	Suite for String Orchestra	G. Schirmer
Delius-Fenby	Air and Dance	Boosey & Hawkes
Johns	Medieval Suite	Henri Elkan
Mozart	Eine Kleine Nachtmusik	Kalmus

ORCHESTRA

Easy

Brahms-Seredy	Hungarian Dances 3 and 6	C. Fischer
Dalley, arr.	American Folk Scene	Hansen
Elgar-Akers	Pomp and Circumstance	C. Fischer
Gluck-Reibold	Hymn to Diana	Fox
Hansen	Little Norwegian Suite	Boosey & Hawkes
Kindler	Three 17th Century Dance Tunes	C. Fischer
Luther-McLin	A Mighty Fortress	Pro Art
McKay	Scenes from the Southwest	Remick
Mussorgsky	Cossack Dance	C. Fischer

Medium

Bergsma	Paul Bunyan Suite	C. Fischer
Dasch	Colonial Dance	FitzSimons
Enesco-Herfurth	Roumanian Rhapsody No. 1	C. Fischer
Glière-Isaac	Russian Sailor's Dance	C. Fischer
Gould	Hill-Billy	C. Fischer
Haydn-Stone	Divertimento	Boosey & Hawkes
Matesky	When Johnny Comes Marching Home	Kjos
Offenbach-Dorati	La Vie Parisienne	Mills
Sibelius-Sopkin	Finlandia	C. Fischer

Difficult

Bruch	Kol Nidrei	G. Schirmer
Cadman	American Suite	Henri Elkan
Copland	An Outdoor Overture	Boosey & Hawkes
Dvořák-Szell	Slavonic Dance No. 1, 3, or 10	Boosey & Hawkes
Grainger	Molly on the Shore	G. Schirmer
Saint-Saëns	Danse Macabre	C. Fischer
Swinach	Danza Andaluza	Peer Int.
Tchaikovsky-Sopkin	Capriccio Italienne	C. Fischer

BAND

Easy

Beethoven-Tolmage	Hymn of Brotherhood	Staff
Borodin-Gardner	Polvetsian Dance	Staff
Erickson	Irish Folk Song Suite	Bourne
Gervaise-McLin	Two Early French Dances	C. Fischer
Keller-Havlicek	American Hymn	Pro Art
Sibelius-Goldman	Onward, Ye Peoples	Galaxy

Medium

Borodin-Cacavas	Polvetsian Dances Theme	Bourne
Christiansen-Watson	First Norwegian Rhapsody	Witmark
Coreili-Suchoff	Dance Suite for Band	Bourne
Lecuona	Bolero Espanol	Marks
Sibelius-Goldman	Karelia Suite, Intermezzo	Associated
Seigmeister, arr.	Five American Folk Songs	C. Fischer
Strauss-Isaac	Gay Vienna Ballet Suite	C. Fischer
Stravinsky-Gardner	*Petrushka* Themes	Staff

Difficult

Copland	Variations on a Shaker Melody	Boosey & Hawkes
Dvořák-Hawkins	*New World Symphony*, Largo	Robbins
Gould-Bennett	Cowboy Rhapsody	Mills
Grundman	Music for a Carnival	Boosey & Hawkes
Grofé-Hawkins	Hendrick Hudson, "Hudson River Suite"	Robbins
Ippolitov-Ivanov	Caucasian Sketches	C. Fischer
Jacob	Music for a Festival	Boosey & Hawkes
Stravinsky	Circus Polka	Associated

BRASS CHOIR

Easy

Gabrieli	Sonata pian' e forte	Elkan-Vogel
Pezel	Sonatas No. 1 and No. 3	R. King

Medium

Cowell	Fanfare for Forces of Latin American Allies	Boosey & Hawkes
Josquin	Motet and Royal Fanfare	R. King
Pezel	Sonata No. 2	R. King

Difficult

Copland	Fanfare for the Common Man	Boosey & Hawkes
Gabrieli	Canzon quarti toni	R. King
Handel	Three Pieces from the *Water Music*	R. King

VOCAL ENSEMBLE

Easy

Hassler	Dancing and Springing	C. Fischer
Mozart	Ave Verum	Spratt
Sullivan	Sing a Merry Madrigal	Boston
Vaughan Williams	O Taste and See	Oxford

Medium

Bach	Jesu, Priceless Treasure	Kjos, G. Schirmer
Purcell	In These Delightful Pleasant Groves	Gray
Purcell	With Drooping Wings	E. C. Schirmer
Ravenscroft	New Oysters	See *An English Song Book*

Difficult

Hindemith	Since All Is Passing	Associated

CHORUS

Easy

Kraft	Festival Song	Mercury
Vree, arr.	Poor Wayfaring Stranger	Presser
Wilson	Our Land	Flammer
Wright, arr.	Men of Harlech	SHM

Medium

Amerman, arr.	Kum Ba Yah	Flammer
Bright	Solomon Grundy	Presser
Chopin-Landau	Three Polish Sons	Choral Art
Churchill, arr.	I'm a Rollin'	Belwin
Kodály	See the Gipsies	Oxford
Ward	Concord Hymn	Mercury

Difficult

Bright	Rainsong	Associated
Copland	That's the Idea of Freedom	Summy-Birchard
Kastle	Three Whale Songs from *Moby Dick*	Colombo
Wykes	Four American Indian Lyrics	Presser

BIBLIOGRAPHY

Barzun, Jacques. *Music in American Life.*
Bulfinch, Thomas. *Mythology of Greece and Rome.*
Ellinwood, Leonard. *The History of American Church Music.*
Farnsworth, Paul R. *The Social Psychology of Music.*
Hume, Paul. *Catholic Church Music.*
Meyer, Leonard B. *Emotion and Meaning in Music.*
Mueller, John H. *The American Symphony Orchestra.*
Music Research Foundation. *Music and Your Emotions.*
Pater, Walter. *The Renaissance.*
Portnoy, Julius. *Music in the Life of Man.*
Rader, Melvin. *A Modern Book of Esthetics.*

(Detailed bibliographical information on these items will be found in the bibliography at the end of this book.)

Content Area 8

MUSIC AS A FORM OF EXPRESSION

Experiences All Music Classes Should Provide

As an art form music is concerned with expressing man's feeling. Since it expresses feelings in a unique way, students, in order to understand this method of expression, must be provided with opportunities to:

1. Discover that music, since earliest times, has been a means through which man has communicated deep feelings and emotions which are related to some of his most important needs.

2. Realize, through the study of music, aesthetic values which are of great value to man.

3. Discover that, unlike the other arts, music exists in time rather than in space, that it must be heard to be ex-

perienced, and remembered to be comprehended in its entirety.

4. Discover *what* music expresses—the emotional response which music evokes in listeners.

5. Discover that music can arouse a wide range of varied feelings—playful, tender, serene, exciting, tragic, humorous, powerful, ironic—giving a satisfying outlet to some of man's deepest emotions.

6. Discover *how* music expresses. This discovery involves intellectual responses.

7. Discover the ways in which the elements of music are used to effect its expressiveness.

8. Discover that though music can sometimes suggest a story or a picture, or express strong feelings, all music fundamentally communicates through its own unique language its own unique content, which is purely musical.

Special Experiences for Nonselective Music Classes

In music classes where performance is not a major objective, students may be helped to understand what it is that music expresses if they are encouraged to:

1. Make a list of the various moods expressed by the music sung or heard in class.

2. Note the various ways in which folk music has been and is today related to man's fundamental needs as expressed in everyday life.

3. List pieces of music that they sincerely like—that they would miss from their life if the music could never be heard again. Each student might try to analyze what it is that this music does for him.

4. Find words used in explaining the content or structure of music, such as color, line, or pattern, which are also used in explaining the content or structure of other arts.

5. Find words which are unique to explaining the content or structure of music.

6. Experiment with developing rhythmic accompaniments that are appropriate to the expressive content of a song.

7. Develop the ability to remember themes in listening to music as an aid to understanding form.

8. Discover that music (unlike literature, painting or sculpture, which seldom have a practical or utilitarian "function") can be both "functional" and "non-functional" while architecture is almost always functional.

9. Discover areas of contemporary life in which music has a "functional" use. What makes it "functional"? What is expressed?

10. Sit through a movie a second time with eyes closed and attempt to follow the plot by the expressive quality of the background music.

11. Use the tape recorder to evaluate the attempts of the class to sing "expressively" such songs as lullabies, patriotic songs, hymns of praise, limericks.

12. Listen to two very expressive musical selections with the same general title and compare the ways each composer handles the musical elements (e.g., "Nocturne" from *Midsummer Night's Dream* by Mendelssohn; *Clair de Lune* of Debussy; *Nocturne* by Grieg; *Night Soliloquy* by Kent Kennan; "Pastorale" from *Christmas Concerto* of Corelli; "Pastorale Symphony" from *Messiah* by Handel; and *The Afternoon of a Faun* by Debussy).

Special Experiences for Instrumental Music Classes

Students in instrumental classes should be assisted in discovering the expressive aspects of the music performed in their classes. They should be encouraged to try to give sincerity and authenticity to all aspects of a performance. Band and orchestra directors are referred to the *Experiences All Music Classes Should Provide* and encouraged to devise ways to bring about these discoveries in their rehearsals. Examples of materials that might be used for such learnings follow:

ORCHESTRA

Easy

Clementi-Sopkin	Sonatina #1	C. Fischer
MacDowell-Isaac	To a Wild Rose	C. Fischer

Medium

Bartók-McKay	Six Pieces for Younger Orchestra	Remick
Debussy-Gordon	Clair de Lune	Elkan-Vogel
Mendelssohn-Reibold	Nocturne	Fox

Difficult

Copland	An Outdoor Overture	Boosey & Hawkes
Glière	Russian Sailor's Dance	Associated

BAND

Easy

Handel-Rebmann	Handel Suite	G. Schirmer
Ortone, arr.	Londonderry Air	Pro Art

Medium

Bartók-Leidzen	An Evening in the Village	Associated
Enesco-Gardner	Roumanian Rhapsody	Staff

Difficult

Beethoven-Roberts	Coriolan Overture	C. Fischer
Christiansen	First Norwegian Rhapsody	Witmark

Special Experiences for Vocal Music Classes

Students in vocal classes should be encouraged to discover the expressive aspects of the music they sing and to develop the techniques for exhibiting expression in performance. Choral directors are referred to the *Experiences All Music Classes Should Provide* and encouraged to invent ways of making their rehearsals laboratories for investigation into musical expression. Sample materials that might be used to develop these capacities follow:

CHORAL—SSA

Easy

Bell, arr.	Now the Day Is Over	Mills
Tchesnokoff	Let Thy Holy Presence	Pro Art

Medium

Clokey	Blue Are Her Eyes	Summy-Birchard
Mozart	Lacrymosa	G. Schirmer

Difficult

Handel	How Excellent Thy Name	Witmark
Pyle	The Fall	C. Fischer

CHORAL—SATB

Easy

Bach	Break Forth O Beauteous Heavenly Light	G. Schirmer
Murray	There Is a Layde	C. Fischer

Medium

Billings-Siegmeister	David's Lamentation	C. Fischer
Bright	The Stars Are With the Voyager	Shawnee

Difficult

Bach	All Breathing Life	G. Schirmer
Vaughan Williams	O Clap Your Hands	Galaxy

BIBLIOGRAPHY

Copland, Aaron. *What To Listen For in Music.*

Earhart, Will. *The Meaning and Teaching of Music.*

Hartshorn, William C., and Helen S. Leavitt. *Making Friends with Music Series.*

McGehee, Thomasine C., (rev. by) Alice D. Nelson. *People and Music.*

Meyer, Leonard B. *Emotion and Meaning in Music.*

Mursell, James L. *Music Education: Principles and Programs.*

Mursell, James L. *The Psychology of Music.*

North Carolina Department of Public Instruction. *Consumer Music for High Schools.*

Portland Public Schools. *A Course in the Understanding of Music.*

Schoen, Max. *Art and Beauty.*

Schoen, Max. *The Understanding of Music.*
Seashore, Carl E. *In Search of Beauty in Music.*
Walter, Bruno. "Of Expression," *Of Music and Music Making.*

(Detailed bibliographical information on these items will be found in the bibliography at the end of this book.)

Content Area 9

TYPES OF MUSICAL PERFORMANCE

The potential of music as an expressive medium is enhanced by the range of types and forms that musical performance includes. The performance of music may be either individual or social. The "society" of performers may range from the solo performer accompanied by a single other performer (accompanist) to the large orchestra, band, or chorus in which the individual performer may play or sing a solo part, may be a member of a small ensemble within the larger ensemble or may be an individual performer contributing his hundredth part to a unified choral or instrumental effect.

MUSIC COMPOSED FOR
LARGE PERFORMING ORGANIZATIONS

Experiences All Music Classes Should Provide

Much of the great music of our heritage has been composed for ensembles involving relatively large numbers of performers. In order to esteem this heritage more fully, students should have:

1. Experiences that will lead to comprehension of the proportionate instrumentation of the modern symphony orchestra and the band.

2. Opportunities to observe the difference in instrumentation between orchestras and wind bands.

3. Familiarity with the range, timbre, and possible voicings of the orchestral and band instruments.

4. An introduction to full orchestral and band scores.

5. Some understanding of the historical development of the modern orchestra—from the use of instruments to double voice parts, the orchestra of the Bach period, the use of interesting and unexpected passages on the flutes, oboes, and bassoons by Rameau, the dramatic resources developed by the Mannheim Orchestra, the extended use of the clarinet and trombone by Mozart, to the expanded instrumentation of Beethoven and contemporary composers.

6. Some understanding of the historical and traditional functions and development of the wind band—uses of trumpets in Biblical times, the rise of the military band as being coeval with the development of organized armies in the 15th and 16th centuries, the infantry regimental bands of Napoleon, the contributions of Adolphe Sax.

7. Acquaintance with the most common forms of literature written for and performed by orchestras: symphony, tone poem, overture, orchestral prelude, dance suite, concerto, and concerto grosso.

8. Appreciation of the symphony orchestra as the instrumental organization for which so much of the great music of the past two hundred years has been written.

9. Appreciation of the contemporary band as a versatile musical organization capable of playing music of all types and styles.

10. Acquaintance with representative band literature for brass band, military band, symphonic band, and wind ensemble.

11. Familiarity with and ability to distinguish between the classifications of male and female voices.

12. Acquaintance with the common vocal conformations —the boys' choir, women's chorus, male and mixed quartet, men's chorus, a cappella mixed choir, antiphonal chorus, large chorus.

13. An understanding of the uses of sacred and secular choral music.

14. Acquaintance with the principal forms of choral composition such as the hymn, madrigal, anthem, motet, cantata, oratorio, opera, chant, part song, etc.

Special Experiences for Nonselective Music Classes

Students in those classes in which performance of the music is not a major concern can further their understanding of the various types of musical performance when they:

1. Become familiar with all the performing organizations in the school and community.

2. Analyze the types of music performed by organizations in the school and community.

3. Analyze the programs of local or visiting symphony orchestras to gain a better understanding of the relative importance of forms of composition. If local groups do not provide sufficient evidence use newspapers (New York Times), magazines (High Fidelity/Musical America), and radio broadcasts (New York Philharmonic). (See Content Area 11, Music Today.)

4. Learn how our notational system symbolizes pitch characteristics of the voices and instruments by means of clefs and transpositions. (See Content Area 4, The Musical Score).

5. Observe the structural elements of musical compositions through listening and score analysis.

6. List well-known compositions in the principal forms of instrumental and choral composition; listen to live or recorded performances of as many of these as possible.

7. Observe the nature of works originally written for band compared with those composed for the orchestra.

8. Work with performing groups on the preparation of assembly programs to demonstrate musical forms and styles; write program notes.

Some music classes in secondary school will be frankly historical in conception. Even those which take a much broader approach may find some helpful suggestions from Content Area 6 and from the following suggestions of compositions to be used in studying types of musical performance.

ORCHESTRA

Early Uses of Instruments

Gabrieli   Sacrae Symphoniae I (1597), a set of compo-
                        sitions often using specific instruments for
                        each part—voices, cornetti, trombones, bas-
                        soons, and violins.

The Late Baroque Orchestra

J. S. Bach   Cantata No. 119, *"Preise, Jerusalem, den
                        Herrn,"* (1723), utilizing 4 voice parts, 4
                        trumpets, 2 timpani, 2 flutes, 3 oboes, 2
                        oboi da caccia, first violins, second violins,
                        viola, and continuo—the latter to be played
                        by violoncelli and organ or harpsichord.
J. S. Bach   Any of the four Orchestral Suites

Mannheim Orchestra

selected compositions of Johann or Karl Stamitz or Cannabich

The Classic Orchestra

Haydn   Symphony No. 94 in G Major ("Surprise")
Haydn   Symphony No. 100 in G Major ("Military")
Mozart   Eine Kleine Nachtmusik
Mozart   Symphony No. 40 in g minor
Mozart   Symphony No. 41 in C Major

The Modern Orchestra

Beethoven   Symphony No. 5 in c minor
Beethoven   Symphony No. 6 in F Major
Beethoven   Symphony No. 9 in d minor
                        (includes vocal chorus)
Berlioz   Roman Carnival Overture
Liszt   Les Preludes (also can be used as an example
                        of the Symphonic Poem)
Mahler   Eighth Symphony (an example of extended
                        use of instruments and the inclusion of vocal
                        choruses)

The Contemporary Orchestra

Compare instrumentation required by Stravinsky's "Rite of Spring"
with instrumentation required by "Histoire du Soldat"—1 violin, 1
double bass, 1 clarinet, 1 bassoon, 1 cornet, 1 trombone, and 2 percussion instruments.

Villa-Lobos   Bachianas Brasileiras No. 5 (eight solo celli
                        and soprano)

BAND

Early Music for the Wind Band

Haydn   Turkish March
Locke   Music for the Coronation of Queen Mary

Mozart	Serenade (K. 361)
Pezel	Tower Sonatas
Purcell	Funeral Music for Queen Mary
Reiche	Tower Sonatas

Band Music of the Nineteenth Century

Berlioz	Grande Symphony Funebre et Triomphale
Gossec	Classic Overture in C
Gossec	Symphony in F
Hummel	Three Grand Military Marches
Mendelssohn	Military Overture, Op. 24
Saint-Saëns	Orient et Occident
Tchaikovsky	Marche Militaire
Wagner	Huldigungsmarsch

Band Music of the Twentieth Century

Busch	A Chant from the Great Plains
Cowell	Celtic Set
Cowell	Shoonthree
Fauchet	Symphony in Bb
Grainger	Children's March
Grainger	Gumsacker's March (with piano)
Grainger	Irish Tune
Grainger	Lads of Wamphray
Grainger	Lincolnshire Posy
Grainger	Shepherd's Hey
Grainger	Spoon River
Holst	First Suite for Band in Eb
Holst	Second Suite for Band in F
Milhaud	Suite Français
Milhaud	West Point Suite
Persichetti	Divertimento for Band
Persichetti	Pageant
Persichetti	Psalm for Band
Vaughan Williams	English Folksong Suite
Vaughan Williams	Toccata Marziale

(Note: The above list indicates the attention given by established composers to the band as a performance medium.)

Marches of Different Nationalities

Alford	Colonel Bogey (England)
Bagley	National Emblem (U.S.A.)
Cray (arr.)	Akebano (Japan)
Delle Case	Inglesina (Italy)
Postal	Flieger (Germany)
Sousa	Stars and Stripes Forever (U.S.A.)
Taxidor	Amparito Roca (Spain)

CHORUS

Renaissance

Lassus	Ich Amer Mann, Lied
Monteverdi	Ecco mormoran l'onde, Madrigal
Palestrina	Missa Papae Marcelli
Josquin des Pres	Ave Maria, Motet. See *Masterpieces of Music Before 1750*

Baroque

Bach	*B Minor Mass*
Bach	*Wachet Auf*, Cantata 140
Crüger	Now Thank We All Our God
Handel	*Messiah*
Monteverdi	*Orfeo*
Purcell	*Dido and Aeneas*
Schütz	*Christmas Story*
Schütz	*Seven Last Words*

Classic

Beethoven	Ninth Symphony
Gay	*Beggars Opera*
Gluck	*Orfeo ed Euridice*
Haydn	*The Creation*
Mozart	*The Magic Flute*
Rossini	*Barber of Seville*

Romantic

Bizet	*Carmen*
Bortniansky	Praise Ye the Lord of Heaven
Brahms	Song of Destiny, and part songs
Glinka	Cherubim Song
Gretchaninov	Glory to God
Mendelssohn	*Elijah*
Schubert	*Mass in E♭*
Strauss	*Der Rosenkavalier*
Verdi	*Aida*
Verdi	*Requiem*
Wagner	*Die Meistersinger*

Twentieth Century

Berg	*Wozzeck*
Britten	Spring Symphony
Dello Joio	*Hymn of Praise*
Gershwin	*Porgy and Bess*
Hindemith	Six Chansons
Kodály	*Psalmus Hungaricus*
Loesser	*The Most Happy Fella*
Poulenc	*Mass*
Stravinsky	Symphony of Psalms
Walton	*Belshazzar's Feast*

Special Experiences for Instrumental Music Classes

Students who are members of school instrumental organizations can further their understanding of types of performance, if they are encouraged to:

1. Demonstrate the range, timbre, and other characteristics of orchestral and band instruments; plan assembly programs of this nature for the whole school.

2. Demonstrate the choirs and effective combinations of instruments within the orchestra and band through playing selected excerpts.

3. Perform the principal forms of orchestral and band literature. Parallel experiences for this activity might involve the use of recordings, concert attendance, observation of musical scores, study of concert programs. A valuable practice for members of the band is the comparison of band transcriptions with original orchestral scores of compositions being performed.

4. List well-known works representing the principal forms of composition for orchestra and band; play or hear as many of these as possible.

5. Relate the music they play to the society and historical period which produced it. (See Content Area 6.)

6. Study the development of the modern orchestra by playing music written for Baroque, Classic, Romantic, and twentieth century orchestras; use scores and recordings to further this understanding.

7. Study the compositions played in orchestra or band by identifying the principal and secondary themes and the instruments to which they are assigned; demonstrate musical structure for other students in the school showing both homophonic and polyphonic uses of thematic material. (See Content Area 2.)

8. Compose, arrange, or transcribe music for the instruments of the band or orchestra.

9. Study the acoustical principles involved in the construction of wind and string instruments; utilize these principles in solving tuning and intonation problems.

10. Analyze the differences between compositions for band and those for orchestra by recognized serious composers who have written specifically for band.

11. Examine compositions performed to determine their potential as transcriptions for other performance media.

12. Participate in the performance of musical compositions for chorus and instrumental accompaniment.

The following are examples of materials that might be used with school instrumental groups to study forms and styles of composition.

ORCHESTRA

Easy

Bartók	Five Pieces for Younger Orchestras	Remick
Gluck	Air de Ballet from *Alceste*	C. Fischer
Handel	Bourrée (strings)	Remick
Handel	Sarabande	C. Fischer
Haydn	Minuet (strings)	Associated
Reed	March of the Prefects	Boosey & Hawkes
Reigger	Suite for Younger Orchestras	Associated
Verrall	Symphony for Young Orchestras	Boston

Medium

Bach	Fugue in g minor	Remick
Beethoven	Ruins of Athens Overture	Broude
Brahms	Hungarian Dance, No. 5	Ditson
Haydn	London Symphony	C. Fischer
Lully	French Baroque Suite	Witmark
Mennin	Sinfonia	Hargail
Stevens	Suite for Small Orchestra	Am. Comp. All.

Difficult

Bach	Brandenburg Concerto No. 3	Broude
Beethoven	*Egmont*, Overture	C. Fischer
Beethoven	Symphony No. 1	Kalmus
Delius-Beecham	The Walk to the Paradise Garden	Boosey & Hawkes
Dvořák	New World Symphony	Kalmus
Haydn-Stoessel	"Emperor" variations (strings)	C. Fischer
Liszt	Hungarian Rhapsody No. 2	G. Schirmer
Massenet	Phedre Overture	Kalmus
Mendelssohn	Italian Symphony	C. Fischer
Prokofiev	Classical Symphony	Kalmus

Saint-Saëns	Danse Macabre	C. Fischer
Sibelius	Karelia Suite, Op. 11	G. Schirmer
Tchaikovsky	Capriccio Italienne	C. Fischer
Wagner	Siegfried Idyll	Associated

BAND

Easy

Carter	Miniature Chorale and Fugue	Hansen
Handel-Rebmann	Handel Suite	G. Schirmer
MacDowell	To a Wild Rose	SHM, Staff
Persichetti	Bagatelles for Band	Elkan-Vogel
Reed	Chorale Prelude in e minor	Hansen
Zaninelli	Hymn and Variations	Shawnee

Medium

Bach-Cailliet	Prelude and Fugue in g minor	C. Fischer
Barber	Commando March	G. Schirmer
Couperin-Gardner	La Sultane Overture	Staff
German-Leidzen	Three Dances, *Nell Gwynn*	Chappell
Handel	Royal Fireworks Music	Century
Stravinsky-Gardner	Berceuse	Staff
Weinberger	Czech Rhapsody	Mercury

Difficult

Beethoven	*Egmont,* Overture	Boosey & Hawkes
Bernstein-Beeler	Overture to *Candide*	G. Schirmer
Copland	Variations on a Shaker Melody	Boosey & Hawkes
Grainger	Hill Song No. 2	Leeds
Holst	Suite 1 and 2	Boosey & Hawkes
Meyerbeer	Fackeltanz	Presser
Mozart-Slocum	*Marriage of Figaro,* Overture	Mills
Riegger	Dance Rhythms	Associated
Williams	Concertino for Percussion and Band	Summy-Birchard

Special Experiences for Vocal Music Classes

Students who are members of school vocal groups can further their understanding of types of musical performance through opportunities to:

1. Perform all types of choral music within the capabilities of the group; prepare assembly programs for the school to demonstrate choral music as a particular type of musical performance.

2. Study the ways in which musical ideas are developed in different types of vocal composition. (e.g., Determine the relationship of voice to accompaniment, importance of solo passages, influence of text on formal design, or any existing imitation between voice parts.) (See Content Area 2.)

3. Study compositions which are performed to determine whether they might be more suitable if arranged for different voice combinations. (e.g., Why are some compositions more suitable for unison performance than for part singing? Why did Bach write verse II of his Cantata 140 (Sleepers Wake) for tenor chorus?)

4. Study compositions which are performed to determine whether they are more suitable for large or small vocal groups. (e.g., Why are some compositions suited ideally for a small group and others for a large chorus?)

5. Participate in the classification of voices within the group.

6. Relate the music they sing, and to which they listen, to the society and historical period which gave it birth.

7. List well-known works representing the principal forms of choral composition; sing or hear as many of them as possible.

8. Participate in the performance of musical compositions for chorus and instrumental accompaniment.

The following are examples of materials that could be used with school vocal groups to study the forms and styles of composition.

CHORUS

Easy

Bach	Break Forth O Beauteous Heavenly Light (SATB)	Wood
Barber	A Nun Takes the Veil (SSA)	Galaxy
Bartholomew (arr.)	Steal Away (TTBB)	G. Schirmer

Christiansen	God Is My Salvation (SATB)	Kjos
Copland	I Bought Me a Cat (TTBB)	Boosey & Hawkes
Farrant-Hilton	Lord, For Thy Tender Mercies Sake (SATB)	E. C. Schirmer
Schubert	Sanctus (SATB)	Staff
Thiman	A Song of Spring (SA)	Novello
Willan	Rejoice Greatly (SA)	Concordia

Medium

Arcadelt	Ave Maria (TTBB)	Bourne
Brahms	Six Folk Songs (SATB)	Marks
Buxtehude	Rejoice Beloved Christian (SATB), cantata	Gray
Gibbons	Almighty and Everlasting God (SATB)	C. Fischer
Humperdinck-Elsmith	Hansel and Gretel (SA)	Summy-Birchard
Kodály	Soldier's Song (TBB)	E. C. Schirmer
Morley	Now Is the Month of Maying (SATB)	Gray
Mozart	Alleluia, from motet *Extultate Jubilate* (SSA)	C. Fischer
Palestrina	Veni Creator (SATB)	C. Fischer
Pergolesi	*Stabat Mater* (SA)	C. Fischer
Purcell	*Dido and Aeneas* (SATB)	Oxford
Purcell	Ode to St. Cecilia (TBB)	C. Fischer
Schubert	*Mass in G* (SATB)	G. Schirmer
Sullivan	*Trial by Jury* (SATB)	Summy-Birchard
Sweelink	O Most High and Holy God (SATB)	SHM
Thompson	The Testament of Freedom (TTBB)	E. C. Schirmer
Vaughan Williams	Prayer to the Father of Heaven (SATB), motet	C. Fischer
Villa-Lobos	Mass in Honor of St. Sebastian (SSA)	Associated
Weill	*Down in the Valley* (SATB)	G. Schirmer
Wilder	*Sunday Excursion* (SATB)	G. Schirmer

Difficult

Bach	Jesu, Joy and Treasure (SSATB), motet	C. Fischer
Brahms	*A German Requiem* (SATB)	C. Fischer
Britten	*A Ceremony of Carols* (SSA)	Boosey & Hawkes
Handel	*Messiah* (SATB)	G. Schirmer

| Holst | Dirge for Two Veterans (TTBB) | E. C. Schirmer |
| Mendelssohn | *Elijah* (SATB) | G. Schirmer |

CHAMBER MUSIC AND SOLOS

Experiences All Music Classes Should Provide

Music composed for only a few instruments or voices may contain some of a composer's greatest thoughts. Since these compositions are apt to be less programmatic and more purely musical in their conception, students will need much opportunity to:

1. Observe the principal characteristic of chamber music —the emphasis on the equal importance of the parts.

2. Hear the various combinations of instruments or voices traditionally used together—string quartet, woodwind quintet, brass ensembles, madrigal groups, male quartet, solo instruments and voices with piano accompaniment, dixieland "combo," etc.

3. Observe the use of the solo performer to express personal and often intense emotions.

4. Compare performances of a given solo by different instruments or by male and female voices.

5. Observe the use of a particular voice or instrument to portray particular emotions or dramatic effects.

6. Observe the completeness of certain instruments (harpsichord, piano, harp, guitar, organ) in the respect that a single performer on a single instrument can provide all the essential components of music—rhythm, melody, and harmony (produced either contrapuntally or homophonically).

7. Study the relationship of keyboard instruments as accompaniments for other instruments that usually play only a single melodic line.

8. Observe the use of the solo voice or instrument in the display of virtuosity.

9. Hear the principal forms of composition for solo instruments and for the standard combinations used in chamber music.

10. Hear various types of solo vocal music such as folk song, pseudo folksong, art song, lieder, and aria.

11. Observe the uses of the solo voice in larger vocal forms such as the Mass, cantata, oratoria, opera, and musical comedy.

12. Become familiar with the major chamber groups, vocal, and instrumental soloists of the contemporary scene. Such familiarity should include the make-up of the groups, the names and typical repertoire of the performers.

Special Experiences for Nonselective Music Classes

Students in music classes in which performance of music is not a major objective can gain a better understanding of music written for small groups or for soloists by having an opportunity to:

1. Discover how many and what kind of chamber music groups exist in the community.

2. Discover the types of music performed by chamber music groups.

3. Examine the scores of chamber music or music for soloists while listening to the music.

4. Listen to soloists from school or community who come to class to demonstrate.

5. Listen to larger musical forms which involve soloists—concertos, cantatas, oratorios, opera, musical comedy.

6. Study scores and listening to performances of solo works which demonstrate the technical versatility required of musicians.

7. Examine newspaper and magazine reviews of performances of soloists with special attention to repertory.

8. Prepare program notes for performances of school soloists.

There follows a brief suggested list of musical examples that might be used in nonselective classes in the study of chamber music and music written for soloists. Where possible musical scores and recordings should be used together. Some of the vocal chamber music may be sung in class.

CHAMBER MUSIC

Instrumental Chamber Music

Debussy	Quartet
Franck	Sonata for Violin and Piano
Haydn	Variations from Emperor Quartet, Op. 76, No. 3
Mendelssohn	Octet for Strings
Mozart	Clarinet Quintet, K. 581
Mozart	Quintet, Winds and Piano, K. 452
Rimsky-Korsakov	Quintet in B flat
Schubert	Trout Quintet, Op. 114
Telemann	Quartet for Winds and Continuo

Vocal Chamber Music

Brahms	Six Folk Songs	Marks
Bartholomew, ed.	Early English Glees (TBB)	Mercury
Bronson	Catches and Glees of the Eighteenth Century	U. of California Press
Christiansen-Pitts, ed.	The Junior A Cappella Chorus Book	Ditson
Greenberg, ed.	An English Song Book	Doubleday
Haydn	The Holy Ten Commandments (Canons)	Mercury
Reichenbach, ed.	Classic Canons	Mercury
Reichenbach, ed.	Easy Canons	Mercury

RECORDINGS

Deller Consort	The English Madrigal School	Vanguard
Deller Consort	English and French Songs of the 16th and 17th Centuries	Westminster
Deller Consort	Italian and Spanish Songs of the 16th and 17th Centuries	Westminster
Mozart	Twelve Canons	Archive
Mozart	Netherlands Chamber Choir	Epic
New York Pro Musica	An Evening of Elizabethan Verse and Its Music	Columbia
Telemann	Quartet for Winds and Continuo	Archive

Concertos

Beethoven	Piano Concerto No. 5, Op. 73 (Emperor)
Gershwin	Concerto in F
Haydn	Concerto for Trumpet
Mendelssohn	Concerto for Violin in e minor, Op. 64
Mozart	Concerto for Clarinet, K 622

| Saint-Saëns | Violoncello Concerto No. 1 in a minor |
| R. Strauss | Concertos for French Horn |

Operatic Arias

Soprano

Gounod	Jewel Song from *Faust*
Bizet	Micaela's Aria from *Carmen*
Delibes	Bell Song from *Lakme*
Verdi	Ah fors' e lui from *La Traviata*
Wagner	Dich Teure Halle from *Tannhauser*

Mezzo-Soprano

| Bizet | Habanera from *Carmen* |

Tenor

| Mozart | Il Mio Tesoro from *Don Giovanni* |
| Wagner | Prize Song from *Die Meistersinger* |

Baritone

| Bizet | Toreador Song from *Carmen* |
| Rodgers | Soliloquy from *Carousel* |

Bass

| Mozart | Se vuol ballare from *Marriage of Figaro* |

Recitative

Bach	Part of Christ in *St. Matthew Passion*
Mozart	Operas
Rossini	Operas

Trumpet Fanfare

Beethoven	*Fidelio*, Act II, (arrival of the governor)
Haydn	Military Symphony
Wagner	*Tristan*, Act II (introduction to the first scene)

Organ Prelude

| Brahms | Chorale Preludes, Op. 122 |

Piano Sonata

Selected from works of Mozart, Beethoven, and others.

Special Experiences for Instrumental Music Classes

Students in instrumental classes and performing groups can further their understanding of chamber music and solo literature when they:

1. Form small instrumental ensembles for the performance and study of chamber music.

2. Listen to recordings of chamber music which they are not able to perform; study it, analyse and discuss it.

3. Accompany instrumental and vocal solos performed by other students or by visiting artists.

4. Demonstrate chamber music and music written for solo performance to the student body in assembly programs.

5. Attend concerts featuring soloists and chamber music performers.

[For appropriate music for these purposes see: *Selective Music Lists:* Instrumental and Vocal Solos, Instrumental and Vocal Ensembles, National Interscholastic Music Activities Commission, 1963; *Materials for Miscellaneous Instrumental Ensembles,* Music Educators National Conference, 1960.]

Special Experiences for Vocal Music Classes

Students in vocal classes and performing groups can further their understanding of chamber music and solo literature if they:

1. Form small vocal ensembles for the performance of madrigals, catches, chansons, canons, and other compositions intended for one voice on a part.

2. Sing solo passages in larger works performed by school groups.

3. Demonstrate the nature of vocal solos for the student body in assembly programs.

4. Listen to recordings of famous singers.

5. Build a list of solo masterpieces written for their own voice classifications.

6. Attend concerts featuring soloists or small groups of singers.

7. Study opera. (See next unit.)

MUSIC, DRAMA AND DANCE

Experiences All Music Classes Should Provide

The experiences planned in conjunction with Content Area 10, Relationship of Music to Other Disciplines in the

Humanities, should provide an understanding of types of musical performance connected with the theatre and dance. These experiences should lead to the development of:

1. An understanding of opera as an art enlisting many different arts—music (both instrumental and vocal), drama, poetry, dance, stage-designing, and costuming.

2. An understanding of the use of music in theatre in today's society. (See Content Area 11, Music Today.)

3. Familiarity with contemporary operas and 20th century composers such as Gershwin, Menotti, Stravinsky, Britten, Berg, and Montemezzi.

4. Acquaintance with operetta and musical comedy as developed in America.

5. An understanding of terms pertaining to opera such as "aria," "ballet," "cadenza," "leitmotif," "libretto," "prelude," "prima donna," "overture," and "recitative."

6. An understanding of the distinguishing characteristics of the principal classifications of solo voices as demonstrated in operatic literature: coloratura soprano, lyric soprano, mezzo-soprano, contralto, lyric tenor, dramatic tenor, "Heldentenor," baritone, bass, and basso profundo.

7. An acquaintance with some of the principal standard works from the repertoire of contemporary opera houses; for example, the operas of Mozart, Rossini, Donizetti, Verdi, Bizet, Gounod, Wagner, Puccini and Mussorgsky.

8. An understanding of Wagner's concept of the music drama.

9. Some idea of the historical development of opera.

10. Familiarity with some of the common terms pertaining to the ballet such as "ballerina," "corps de ballet," "fouetta," "grand jetée," "pas de basque," "pas de chat," "pas de deux," "pirouette," "points," etc. Where possible this should be developed in conjunction with demonstrations by students or community resource persons.

11. An understanding of the role of ballet in opera.

12. Acquaintance with the use of ballet in contemporary musical theatre such as *Oklahoma* and *West Side Story*.

13. Familiarity with contemporary ballets and 20th century composers such as Stravinsky, Ravel, Bernstein, Copland, Falla, and Prokofiev.

14. Familiarity with national dance forms such as the Czech polka, Hungarian czardas, Polish krakoviak, Scottish reel, American and Latin American dances, and folk dancing in general.

15. Some understanding of the influence of dancing on musical form as demonstrated by the instrumental dance suite and its elements, the allemande, courante, sarabande, gavotte, minuet, bourrée, and gigue.

16. Familiarity with the types of musical theatre and ballet (both amateur and professional) to be found in the local community.

Special Experiences for Nonselective Music Classes

Students in those classes in which performance of music is not a major concern may develop better understanding of the effectiveness of combining music with theatre and dance through:

1. Comparing a play with an opera that has been made from that play. [e.g., *La Dame aux Camélias* (Dumas) and *La Traviata* (Verdi); *La Tosca* (Sardou) and *Tosca* (Puccini); *Pelléas and Mélisande* (Maeterlinck and Debussy); *Otello* (Shakespeare and Verdi); *Green Grow the Lilacs* (Riggs) and *Oklahoma* (Rodgers and Hammerstein); *Pygmalion* (Shaw) and *My Fair Lady* (Lerner and Loewe); *Taming of the Shrew* (Shakespeare) and *Kiss Me Kate* (Porter).]

2. Studying other literary sources (folk-lore, poetry, novels) on which libretti are based. [e.g., *Carmen* (Mérimée and Bizet); *Down in the Valley* (Weill); *Guys and Dolls* (Damon Runyon and Loesser). Study the texts of Gilbert and Sullivan operettas for evidences of social and political satire.]

3. Comparing subjects, plots and centers of dramatic interest in operas of various composers and of various periods of social history.

4. Exploring opera repertoires of present day companies.

5. Cooperating in school production of music drama. Helping with scenery, programs, costumes, lighting, etc.

6. Exploring the social forces reflected in the development of opera.

7. Becoming familar with local productions (both amateur and professional) that involve music, drama, and the dance.

8. Exploring the societal customs associated with the origin and function of folk and national dance forms.

9. Dancing some of the folk and social dances and then trying to relate them to musical compositions inspired by such dances. (e.g., Study the minuet as a dance and as a movement of a suite or symphony; the waltz as a dance and as the inspiration for a composition such as *Invitation to the Dance* [Weber]; American folk dances and their use in *Rodeo* by Copland.)

10. Studying American jazz as the development of music for dancing and its effect on serious musical composition. Pursuing questions such as how much limitation the continuing $\frac{4}{4}$ meter of earlier jazz placed on the serious composer who wished to employ the idiom. Discovering contemporary jazz that is not limited in this manner.

Special Experiences for Instrumental Music Classes

Members of instrumental performing organizations can further their understanding of the importance of drama and the dance to the development of our musical heritage through:

1. Playing overtures, ballet music, dance suites, and instrumental excerpts from stage productions and studying the background of the music they play.

2. Accompanying soloists and choruses in producing opera, operetta or musical comedy or excerpts from them.

3. Providing the music for ballet productions.

Special Experiences for Vocal Music Classes

Members of vocal performing organizations can further their understanding of music, dance, and the theatre arts by:

1. Singing selections from opera, operetta and musical comedy which are appropriate to their capabilities and studying the background of such music.

2. Demonstrating for each other and for other students various aspects of the combination of singing and dramatic action.

3. Joining forces with other departments—speech, drama, dance, art, home economics, industrial arts—to produce a musical drama.

4. Experimenting with choral—dance productions in co-operation with other students in the school.

BIBLIOGRAPHY

Anderson, Donald. "Survey of Musical Style for Band," *Missouri Journal of Research in Music Education.*

Dilla, Geraldine P. "Music-Drama: An Art Form in Four Dimensions," *The Musical Quarterly.*

Eberhart, Constance. "A select list of operas suitable for performance by school groups."

Fletcher, H. G. "Music Appreciation As an Aid in Band and Orchestra Instruction," *Music Educators Journal.*

Goldman, Richard Franko. *The Wind Band: Its Literature and Technique.*

Green, Douglass M. *Form in Tonal Music.*

Grout, Donald J. "Chronology," *A History of Western Music,* pp. 699-719.

Heffner, H. C. "Theatre and Drama in Liberal Education," *Teachers College Record.*

Hoffer, Charles R. "Selecting Music for School Groups," Chapter XVI in *Teaching Music in the Elementary Schools.*

Jacobs, Arthur. *Choral Music.*

Modisett, Katherine Carpenter. "Bibliography of Sources, 1930-1952, Relating to the Teaching of Choral Music in Secondary Schools," *Journal of Research in Music Education.*

Rensin, Hy. *Basic Course in Music.*

Morie, Wayne. "Principal Instrumental Forms of the Baroque Era," *Missouri Journal of Research in Music Education.*

Richardson, Allen L., and Mary E. English. "Design and Development," *Living with Music,* Vol. I, pp. 91-126.

Richardson, Allen L., and Mary E. English. "Past, Present, and Future," *Living with Music,* Vol. II, pp. 103-123.

Sur, William R., and Charles Francis Schuller. "Music Literature, A Source of Musical Growth," *Music for Teenagers.*

(Detailed bibliographical information on these items will be found in the bibliography at the end of the book.)

Content Area 10

RELATIONSHIP OF MUSIC TO OTHER DISCIPLINES IN THE HUMANITIES

Experiences All Music Classes Should Provide

All students in our schools need to participate in activities which will lead them to discover that the arts serve a basic need of man and have been and continue to be of great importance to him. Such activities might include opportunities to:

1. Analyze the nature of the arts with emphasis on their intrinsic values.

2. Make comparisons among the arts as to their similarities and differences.

3. Observe the principle of repetition and contrast as basic to all of the arts.

4. Explore the ways in which the arts are combined as in opera, ballet, art song, and liturgical music.

5. Discover the elements which are basic to each of the arts, noting those which are unique to each and those which seem to relate to two or more.

6. Develop an understanding that all of the arts stem from the desire on the part of the creator to express something.

Special Experiences for Nonselective Music Classes

Students in music classes which are essentially non-performing should be encouraged to:

1. Attend a ballet to observe the way in which the arts complement one another.

2. Attend a ballet to observe the way in which music and the dance combine toward a common purpose.

3. Listen to music, study a painting and a poem, all of which deal with a similar title or subject, to see how these arts deal with a common idea (e.g., music—*Evening in the Village*, Bartók, and painting—*Evening in the Country*, Dale Nichols, New York Graphic Society; poetry—*Afternoon on a Hill*, Edna St. Vincent Millay, and painting—*Nature's Dreamland*, J. A. Botke, New York Graphic Arts; music—*The White Peacock*, Griffes, and poetry—*The White Peacock*, William Sharpe).

4. Listen to music, study a painting and a poem, all of which were created in the same historical style (e.g., Impressionism—Debussy, composer; Monet, painter; Verlaine, poet—noting the relationships among these three arts which exhibit a certain similarity in techniques).

5. Study such examples of the art song as *The Erlking* by Schubert in order to observe the way in which music and poetry may enhance one another in communicating an intensity of feeling. Other examples of art songs or madrigals which may be sung or played might include *None But the Lonely Heart* by Tchaikovsky, *Morgen* by Richard Strauss, *Dedication* by Franz, or *Now Is the Month of Maying* by Morley.

FILMS

The Renaissance	EBF
Pacific 231	McGraw-Hill

RECORDINGS

The Bells	Rachmaninov
(read poem of Poe by the same name)	
Engulfed Cathedral	Debussy
(see Monet's painting of the same name)	
The Isle of the Dead	Rachmaninov
(see Bochlin's painting with the same name)	
"Prelude" and "Love Death" from *Tristan und Isolde*	Wagner
(read *Tristram* by Edwin Arlington Robinson)	
Pictures at an Exhibition	Mussorgsky
(to be used with Hartmann's pictures)	
Romeo and Juliet, ballet	Prokofiev
Romeo and Juliet, opera	Gounod

Romeo and Juliet Overture   Tchaikovsky
Romeo and Juliet Symphony   Berlioz
   (read portions of Shakespeare's *Romeo and Juliet*)
Sea Drift   Delius
   (to be used with the Whitman poem)

Special Experiences for Instrumental Music Classes

Members of bands, orchestras and other instrumental ensembles should be assisted in the study of poems or pictures related to the music being performed. They should also have the opportunity to become familiar with stories behind operas or musical shows performed in class in order to make more effective interpretations. They should also incorporate ideas inherent in relationships among the arts in their public performances through (a) program notes; (b) introducing, where appropriate, the reading of poems or excerpts from literature; (c) exhibiting art works in the auditorium foyer when concerts are presented; and (d) using audio-visual devices such as projecting slides, when appropriate, which illustrate relationships among the arts.

ORCHESTRA

Easy

Gluck	Air de Ballet from *Alceste*	C. Fischer
Handel- Zamecnik	Minuet from *Berenice*	Fox

Medium

Bizet-Seredy	*Carmen* Selection	C. Fischer
Copland	Waltz from *Billy the Kid*	Boosey & Hawkes

Difficult

Delius-
  Beecham
	The Walk to the Paradise
	  Garden
		Boosey &
		  Hawkes

Tchaikovsky	*Romeo and Juliet* Overture	Kalmus
Grieg	Peer Gynt Suite #1	C. Fischer

BAND

Easy

Isaac-Lillya	A Summer Evening Serenade	Fox
Luther	A Mighty Fortress Is Our God	Staff

Medium

Bernstein- Beeler	Selections, *West Side Story*	G. Schirmer

| Strauss-Davis | Allerseelen | Ludwig |
| Schuman | When Jesus Wept | Merion |

Difficult

| Mussorgsky | Pictures at an Exhibition, Part 2 | C. Fischer |
| Puccini | *La Bohème*, Selections | Ricordi |

Special Experiences for Vocal Music Classes

Members of vocal groups should be assisted in the study of poems or pictures related to the music being performed. They should also have the opportunity to become familiar with stories behind operas or musical shows performed in class in order to make more effective interpretations. They should make a practice of carefully studying the texts used in songs performed, asking the question: Are they appropriate to the music or is the music appropriate to them? They should also incorporate ideas inherent in relationships among the arts in their public performances through (a) program notes; (b) introducing, where appropriate, the reading of poems or excerpts from literature; (c) exhibiting art works in the auditorium foyer when concerts are presented; and (d) using audio-visual devices such as projecting slides, when appropriate, which illustrate relationships among the arts.

CHORAL—SSA

Easy

| Weelkes-Harris | Welcome Sweet Pleasure | Wood |
| Brahms-Gibb | The Quiet Wood | Boston |

Medium

| Elgar-Ehret | The Snow | Choral Art |
| Mendelssohn-Dietrich | O Rest in the Lord | Summy-Birchard |

(can also be sung, as originally written, in unison)

Difficult

| Schubert-Watson | The Lord Is My Shepherd | Remick |
| Persichetti | This Is the Garden | C. Fischer |

CHORAL—SATB

Easy

Beethoven	The Heavens Are Declaring	C. Fischer
Franz	Dedication	Summy-Birchard

(can also be sung, as originally written, in unison)

Medium

Elgar	As Torrents in Summer	Summy-Birchard
Gibbons	The Silver Swan	C. Fischer

Difficult

Mendelssohn	He Watching over Israel	G. Schirmer
Holst	The Heart Worships	Galaxy

BIBLIOGRAPHY

Copland, Aaron. *Music and Imagination.*
Fleming, William. *Arts and Ideas.*
Fleming, William, and Abraham Veinus. *Understanding Music.*
Hartshorn, William C. *Music for the Academically Talented Student in the Secondary School.*
Hartnoll, Phyllis, ed. *Shakespeare in Music.*
McGinn, Donald J., and George Howerton. *Literature As a Fine Art.*
McKinney, Howard, and W. R. Anderson. *Discovering Music.*
Missouri State Department of Education. *The Allied Arts—A High School Humanities Guide.*
Myers, Bernard S. *Understanding the Arts.*
Portnoy, Julius. *Music in the Life of Man.*
Sachs, Curt. *The Commonwealth of Art.*
Stringham, Edwin J. *Listening to Music Creatively.*
Wold, Milo, and Edmund Cykler. *An Introduction to Music and Art in the Western World.*

(Detailed bibliographical information on these items will be found in the bibliography at the end of the book.)

Content Area 11

MUSIC TODAY

Experiences All Music Classes Should Provide

All students can profit from explorations into the function and extent of music in the community (local, national, world) by means of:

1. Interviews with cultural leaders and professional musicians in the local area with written or oral reports to the class.

2. Examination of magazines (*Time, Newsweek, High Fidelity/Musical America, The New Yorker, Saturday Review*) and newspapers (local, and *New York Times* or *Christian Science Monitor*) with written or oral reports to the class.

3. Interviews and/or correspondence with managers of symphony orchestras, opera companies and other musical institutions relative to attendance figures, community support, trends over the past ten years, type of repertoire, etc.

4. Group attendance at specific local concerts followed by class discussion and evaluation of the performance and music heard.

5. Correspondence with government officials relative to support of the arts. (e.g., Students might seek information on state money for concerts by the North Carolina Symphony Orchestra; pending state and national legislation dealing with the arts; the federal government's National Council on the Arts; local governmental support for local institutions.)

6. Correspondence with the Department of State relative to the Cultural Exchange program. A class might study the types of performing groups chosen to represent America and those that have come here from other countries.

7. Collection of statistics relative to concert attendance, sale of music and records, and number of full time musicians employed. Sources of such information that might be used: American Music Conference, Broadcast Music Inc., Music Publishers Association, American Federation of Musicians, U.S. Departments of Labor and Commerce, and the American Symphony Orchestra League.

8. Reading of books and making oral or written reports to class.

9. Preparation of a monthly calendar of events for the local community to include as many of the opportunities to

hear music as possible—school concerts, formal concerts, church services, municipal band concerts, SPEBSQSA contests, amateur and professional theatre groups.

10. Preparation of a schedule of radio and television performances of music of interest to the study of the class.

11. Interviews with composers who might live in community. Special effort should be made to see that students come in contact with new ideas in music—chance music, electronic music, and other ways in which twentieth century composers are attempting to be original.

12. Correspondence to determine the position of opera in contemporary America. Sources of information might include the National Opera Association, the Metropolitan Opera Association, and the National Association of Schools of Music.

Other activities leading to a better understanding of music in the life of today might include:

1. Performances in class by adult amateurs and/or professionals in the community.

2. Debates on topics of sociological and musical interest. (e.g., *Resolved:* "That in the United States the composer has greater status than the performer;" or *Resolved:* "That the European practice of government subsidization for the arts is preferable to the United States practice of non-government support.")

3. Visits to class from music critics, music directors of radio stations, officers of the nearest local of the musicians' union.

4. Keeping diaries of contacts made with music in all phases of students' lives.

5. Examination of music as a way of initiating contacts between nationals of different countries. (e.g., Make a study of American opera singers who live abroad while getting experience in small opera houses that do not exist in America.)

6. Study of the international exchange in recordings—serious music, jazz, folk music.

Special Experiences for Nonselective Music Classes

Many of the activities which are listed as basic—surveys, interviews, etc.—should probably be conducted by members of the non-performing music classes and the results shared with the members of the band, orchestra, chorus and ensembles just as these students will contribute to the music classes through demonstration. Other valuable activities might include:

1. Listening to recordings for evidences of "national" characteristics.

2. Listening for evidences of American jazz idiom in the music by composers of other countries.

3. Writing program notes for concerts of contemporary music prepared by school performing groups.

4. Viewing films such as Leonard Bernstein's Moscow and Berlin Concerts available from the Ford Motor Company, or his Children's Concerts being distributed by the American Telephone and Telegraph Company.

Special Experiences for Instrumental Music Classes

Instrumental music study might be expected to include study of biographical data of contemporary composers whose music is played in class.

Students can obtain a better picture of the role of music in today's society through an examination of ways in which school instrumentalists might make additional contributions to the life of the community and through carrying out of such plans.

Students can be assisted in the identification of characteristics of music that can be labeled as "national." Similarly they should be aided in identifying the specific attributes of contemporary music, "neo-classic", etc.

BAND

Easy

| Prokofiev-Lang | Gavotte (from the *Classical Symphony*) | Mills |

Medium

Bartók- Leidzen	An Evening in the Village	Associated
Mersey	Jazz Suite	Fox
Prokofiev- Walters	Troika	Rubank
Sanjuan	Caribbean Sketch	Leeds
Siegmeister	Five American Folk Songs	C. Fischer

Difficult

Chávez	Chapultepec	Mills
Cowell	Hymn and Fuguing Tune No. 1	Leeds
Khachaturian (arr. Satz)	Armenian Dances	Leeds
Siegmeister	Prairie Legend	Broadcast Music
Still	From the Delta, Suite	Leeds
Schoenberg	Theme and Variations for Band	G. Schirmer

ORCHESTRA

Easy

Vaughan
  Williams
  (arr. Jacob)
	English Folk Song Suite	Boosey &
		  Hawkes

Medium

Bergsma	Paul Bunyan Suite	C. Fischer

Copland	"Prairie Night and Celebration"
	  (from *Billy the Kid*)
		Boosey &
		  Hawkes

McKay	Variations on a Texas Tune	G. Schirmer

Difficult

Tomlinson	Suite of English Folk Dances	British- American
Williams	Fantasia on Welsh Nursery Tunes	Oxford

Special Experiences for Vocal Music Classes

Vocal students might be expected to include study of biographical data of contemporary composers whose works are sung in class. They will gain insights from an examination of ways in which school singers might make additional contributions to the life of a community. A profitable project might be the study of relationship between language and the "national" character of vocal music.

A valuable service to the class and to the school might be an inventory of opportunities to hear good choral music in the community with emphasis on contemporary music.

CHORAL—SSA

Easy

Barber	A Nun Takes the Veil	G. Schirmer
Bergsma	Let True Love Among Us Be (SA)	C. Fischer
Donovan	Songs of Nature	Associated
Kodály	Ave Maria	Boosey & Hawkes
Mennin	Bought Locks	C. Fischer
Thompson	Now I Lay Me Down To Sleep	E. C. Schirmer

Medium

Bartók	Enchanting Song	Boosey & Hawkes
Bartók	The Wooing of a Girl	Boosey & Hawkes
Britten	A Ceremony of Carols	Boosey & Hawkes
Kodály	Cease Your Bitter Weeping	Boosey & Hawkes
Schuman	The Lord Has a Child	Presser
Thompson	The Gate of Heaven	E. C. Schirmer

Difficult

Diamond	All in Green My Love Went Riding	So.Mu.Pub.Co.
Dohnanyi	Stabat Mater (SSSAAA)	Associated
Goodman	Lyrics	Mercury
Hindemith	A Song of Music	Associated
McDonald	Evening	Elkan-Vogel
Santa Cruz	Cantares de Pascua (Ten Songs of Christmas)	Peer Int.

CHORAL—TTBB

Easy

Copland	I Bought Me A Cat	Boosey & Hawkes
Gordon	Why So Pale and Wan, Fond Lover	Boosey & Hawkes
Persichetti	Song of Peace	Elkan-Vogel
Vaughan Williams	Let Us Now Praise Famous Men (unison)	G. Schirmer

Medium

Kay	Come Away, Come Away Death	Peer Int.
Kodály	Soldiers Song (TBB)	Boosey & Hawkes
Moore	Simon Legree	C. Fischer
Schuman	Truth Shall Deliver	G. Schirmer
Stevens	Four Carols	Peer Int.
Stravinsky	Four Russian Peasant Songs	Marks
Zolatariev	The Answers	So.Mo.Pub.Co.

Difficult

Barber	A Stopwatch and An Ordnance Map	G. Schirmer
Bartók	Five Slovak Folk Songs	Boosey & Hawkes
Berger	Hope for Tomorrow	G. Schirmer
Cowell	Day, Evening, Night, Morning	Peer Int.
Creston	Two Motets	G. Schirmer
Hindemith	The Demon of the Gibbet	Schott
Piston	Carnival Song	Associated

CHORAL—SATB

Easy

Bingham	The Christmas Man	J. Fischer
Copland	Simple Gifts	Boosey & Hawkes
Cowell	Lilting Fancy	Mercury
McKay	Morning Prayer	SHM
Rowley	Praise	Oxford
Weigel	The Nightwind	Mercury

Medium

Avshalomov	Because Your Voice	Galaxy
Bacon	Jonah	Peer Int.
Barber	Sure on This Shining Night	G. Schirmer
Bartók	Three Hungarian Folk Songs	Boosey & Hawkes
Hindemith	Six Chansons	Associated
Riegger	Who Can Revoke	Marks
Rorem	Sing My Soul	Peters
Shaw	O Clap Your Hands	Novello
Sowerby	I Will Lift Up Mine Eyes	Boston
Thiman	Go, Lovely Rose	Elkin & Co.
Thomson	Follow Thy Fair Son	Colombo
Walton	What Cheer	Oxford

Difficult

Berger	Brazilian Psalm	G. Schirmer
Bergsma	Riddle Me This	C. Fischer

Chávez	Three Nocturnes	G. Schirmer
Dello Joio	Madrigal	C. Fischer
Ives	Let There Be Light	Peer Int.
Kodaly	Jesus and the Traders	Boosey & Hawkes
Martinu	Five Czech Madrigals	Boosey & Hawkes
Mennin	The Gold Threaded Robe	C. Fischer
Milhaud	Cantate de la Guerre	G. Schirmer
Milhaud	Cantate de la Paix	G. Schirmer
Phillips	A Bucket of Water	Elkan-Vogel
Poulenc	Exultate Deo	Colombo
Schoenberg	To Her I Shall Be Faithful	Marks
Stravinsky	Symphony of Psalms	Boosey & Hawkes
Vaughan Williams	The Hundredth Psalm	Galaxy

BIBLIOGRAPHY

Barzun, Jacques. *Music in American Life.*
Bauer, Marion. *20th Century Music.*
Ewen, David. *American Composers Today.*
Hiller, Lejaren A., and Leonard T. Isaacson. *Experimental Music.*
Machlis, Joseph. *Introduction to Contemporary Music.*
Moore, Christopher. "A bibliography of contemporary choral music for high voices, performable by children."
Nettl, Bruno. *An Introduction to Folk Music in the United States.*
Salazar, Adolfo. *Music in Our Time.*
Sessions, Roger. *Reflections on Musical Life in the U.S.*
Smith, Cecil. *Worlds of Music.*
Toffler, Alvin. *The Culture Consumers.*
United States Information Agency. *Catalog of Published Concert Music by American Composers.*

(Detailed bibliographical information on these items will be found in the bibliography at the end of the book.)

CHAPTER V

Utilization of School and Community Resources

"An educated person is aware of his environment," is an observation made in Chapter Two of this book. If the student is to understand "the function of music in the life of the community," it will be necessary for the school to offer musical experiences related to that life. It should be the conscious objective of all staff members concerned with the music program to promote a curiosity about and an awareness of all local musical resources.

COMMUNITY MUSIC RESOURCES

In almost every community in the United States there will be musicians who may be utilized in the school in order to broaden students' musical experiences. These may range from professional singers and instrumentalists who will perform at a school assembly to a shy folk singer who may have to be "taped" in his own home and his music brought back to class. In between is a continuum of semi-professional musicians, parents, and friends who need to be sought out by the music faculty in order that their talents may contribute to the general education of children and thereby raise the cultural level of the community.

A most effective classroom project can involve research and discussion of all the local music resources available to the students including: TV, radio, motion pictures, public concerts, music stores and record shops, newspapers and periodicals, churches, music clubs, mother-singers, musicians' union, museums, community festivals involving music, family music groups, music in industry, local composers and

157

arrangers, folk singers, piano technicians, instrument makers, and amateur performing groups. Bulletin boards (or scrapbooks) of current musical events also serve to make students aware of what is going on around them. Use may be made of the school "dailygram" to publicize concerts (TV, radio, live) or other items of musical interest (lecture, cinema, related reading). Evidence of school interest in musical happenings may help improve situations in which newspapers are not giving adequate coverage to musical events. Classroom discussions of current musical activities can be useful for their own sake or as they relate to the immediate curriculum being studied. The value of attendance at concerts, recitals, and church services can be enhanced by advance preparation in the classroom. Scores or recordings of works to be performed may be analysed or the nature of the service in a particular church explained and the role of music discussed objectively.

Bringing musicians into the school is important. Professional and accomplished amateur musicians may be used for demonstration purposes. Some may play for assembly; others demonstrate correct vocal production for the school chorus. They may conduct sectional rehearsals of the band or orchestra. Chamber music groups may give counsel on the techniques of small ensemble playing. Sound engineers may talk on high-fidelity reproduction systems, stereophonic sound, or acoustics. Local composers may talk to the class or rehearse their own works with a school group. A music librarian might discuss facilities and collections available. Instrumental repair men may advise students regarding the care and maintenance of their instruments. The more adults from the community who can be brought to the school to demonstrate musical interest and talent the better. By this means the student body comes to realize just how extensive is the interest in music in their own immediate environment.

A study of the role of the community in the evolution and development of instrumental music and a similar study of singing would be interesting projects in social studies classes. Possible topics of investigation are: the social nature of primitive instruments, the influence of the church, royal courts and music, the role of the minnesingers and troubadours, the importance of patrons, the influence of wars on the development of music, the allied arts (poetry, theatre, dance), the influence of government, music and education, nationalistic influences, economic influences, the "star" system, scientific advances, private foundations, protective legislation (copyright), artist guilds and musicians' unions, *Gebrauchsmusik*, and the jazz milieu. Music teachers should make such suggestions to the teachers of social studies and be willing to serve as resource persons when the sociology of music is being investigated. Both music teachers and sociologists should help students to see the parallels which may exist between past societies and their own. Actual music related to the topics must be employed if such study is to be anything more than pure social science.

STUDENT MUSICIANS

Student musicians can contribute a great deal toward helping the entire student body realize outcomes of a general education in music. It is a major tenet of this book that this is one of the obligations of the school's performing groups. Programs prepared by the school orchestra and band should contribute to the general education of the school (see Chapter VIII, Promising Practices, p. 184). Music teachers must not only plan their programs for this purpose but must also see that the audience is prepared to benefit by the performance. An assembly program featuring the high school choir singing beautiful and technically difficult music may have little or no educational value to the rest of the student body unless the program is organized around a musical idea or topic with provision made for advance preparation and either oral or written program notes. Exchange concerts with other schools should be scheduled with concern for making them learning situations for performers and audience alike.

Talented individual students also represent a valuable resource pool. They can be used to demonstrate the sound of instruments or types of human voices. They can provide musical illustrations for the study of history, literature, and the other arts. They can demonstrate smaller musical forms such as the aria, sonata, or lied. They can provide a bona fide aesthetic experience for those who listen.

The practice of isolating the rehearsal rooms from the rest of the school is hardly defensible in an institution which is anxious to use its choir, band, or orchestra for educating the student body. Why shield students from the fact that the orchestra is preparing the Mendelssohn "Italian" Symphony for the festival when they are going home to study their geometry in front of the radio? Obviously, no lecturing teacher wants to compete with the volume of the band, but, within reason, the activities of the music department need not be a secret to the rest of the school. There is the further danger that music educators working apart from the mainstream of school life may never achieve the effectiveness they otherwise could.

Music teachers are reminded of the fact that not all the good musicians in the school are necessarily those involved in the school's performing groups. Pianists, especially, may do all of their music study outside the school. A systematic investigation of the musical talent of the student body is often worthwhile, particularly in the larger secondary schools.

FACULTY

Faculty members, both music teachers and others, should not be overlooked as a rich pool of varied talent with value for the program of general education in music. Music teachers frequently do not have a chance to perform in their teaching assignment but might be of service to illustrate musical concepts in other (history or literature) classes or in assemblies. It is even more important that teachers of other subjects who are performers demonstrate this, in order that the students see that music teachers are not the only persons whose education has included music.

The avocational interests of all the teachers in the school should be investigated. In addition to performing abilities, teachers may possess private record collections of special interest. Those who have lived abroad may have knowledge of the music of foreign cultures. Even those teachers without any particular musical training should be encouraged to present a positive attitude toward the subject. The principal who thinks he is supporting the music program by saying "I don't know anything about music but I like it and think the school should have music" might well re-examine his position. It is doubtful that he would make a similar statement about basketball. Musical learnings (and contagious attitudes) are the responsibility of the whole school.

RADIO AND TELEVISION

The general education curriculum of a school should be planned to incorporate the best musical offerings available on radio and television. Class critiques of concerts over these media can be employed in order to develop discriminating listening habits. Listening to local "Good Music Stations" should be encouraged both in school and out. Program guides available from such stations should be utilized not only for their listings and explanatory notes but also as a chronicle of the current musical scene. Opportunities for school performing groups to appear on radio and television should be recognized also as additional occasions for working toward realization of some of the outcomes of Chapter II.

FIELD TRIPS

Field trips into the community may add to the strength of the music program. Group attendance can sometimes be arranged at concerts with the school providing transportation and chaperones. Students should be instructed in appropriate audience decorum beforehand, and prepared for listening to the music to be performed. Other worthwhile trips might be made to music stores, conservatories, or places of unique musical interest such as the shop of a music engraver, an instrument maker, or the home of a composer. Trips to a church to hear and see the organ can be arranged in almost every community. A visit to the radio or television studio may be profitable in some areas. Museums of various types may offer opportunities to examine ancient musical instruments, observe original manuscripts of music scores, or to relate great works of art to music studied in class.

LIBRARY

Libraries in the community should be utilized to the fullest. Music teachers can encourage research in school and public libraries on the part of all types of students. Members of performing organizations can add to the educational experience of the rehearsal by discovering information on the music being played or sung and sharing it with the group. Class assignments can encourage research in the holdings of the libraries or in their collections of recordings. Circulating libraries of phonograph records make it possible to assemble two or three interpretations of a single composition for comparison. This can be a most effective way of developing discrimination on the part of students and can be a way of guiding them in the building of their own personal libraries of recordings.

HOMES

The homes of a community should not be overlooked as a rich source for examples of the type of relationship with music that a general education in music program is attempting to foster. Music teachers should be on the lookout for homes where music is a natural part of family life no matter how simple and informal the music may be. Family music groups that can come to school will demonstrate the human values of a general education in music.

It is probable also that the school will wish to help other families develop the type of home atmosphere which can both foster and profit from general education in music. Many parents will need detailed suggestions as to what to do to bring this about. Arrangements should be made to familiarize the parents with the goals of the program. The school might assemble a loan collection of social instruments which could be borrowed by family units. Arrangements might be made with local libraries to increase their collections of records and music for use by family groups. If there is an adult education program in the community, music courses geared to the family's role in general music education might be arranged. Students in performing groups should be counseled as to the use of their skills with voice or instruments in their own family situation.

Because the desired outcomes in general education in music are precisely those that can contribute to a healthy atmosphere in the home, and because a musical home can do so much to help develop these skills and attitudes in young people, it is strongly urged that school systems do not neglect this resource as they plan their program of musical activities.

CHAPTER VI

Administering the
Music Curriculum

THE development and maintenance of a comprehensive program of music instruction at the secondary school level encompassing the content areas outlined in Chapter IV will require careful planning and administering. The primary task of the persons responsible for organizing the music curriculum, whether they be directors of music, supervisors, principals, or teachers, will be to interpret the broader aims and objectives of this program to the other members of the administrative and teaching staff and to the community at large. This will undoubtedly prove to be more difficult in communities where the musical spotlight has been focussed almost exclusively on the accomplishments of the high school performing groups and their indisputable value as public relations media. Conant's critical study of the American high school,[1] as well as the recent position paper, "The Arts in the Comprehensive Secondary School"[2] of the National Association of Secondary School Principals have helped to pave the way for a shift of emphasis, but a great deal of "selling" remains to be done. To dispel the predominant image will require the utmost tact and ingenuity and the music educator must be prepared to defend his position with sound educational reasons.

The implementation of a broader program of music instruction at the secondary school level will hinge largely on adjustments and modifications in the following broad areas of the administrator's concern.

---

[1] James Conant, *The American High School Today.* (New York: McGraw-Hill Book Company, Inc., 1959.)

[2] National Association of Secondary School Principals, *op. cit.*

THE SCHOOL PLANT

Rehearsal rooms for vocal and instrumental groups, practice rooms, studios, and storage space are provided in most modern secondary schools. *Music Buildings, Rooms, and Equipment*,[3] published by the Music Educators National Conference is an excellent reference in this area. Provision in music rooms for some type of movable partitions to facilitate the grouping of students for special activities and projects is highly desirable.

The use of school performing organizations, both small ensembles and large groups, to give educational concerts or to provide musical illustrations for related areas of study will make special demands on the school plant. Auditoriums may function well for some of these purposes but small recital halls or enlarged classrooms may offer a better solution for others.

The program as suggested in Chapter IV relies heavily on ready accessibility to a comprehensive library of recordings, scores, and other reference materials. Adequate provision for efficient storage of these items must be made either in the music department itself, preferably, or in an instructional materials center serviced by the school library staff. Provisions should also be made to enable individuals to listen to recorded material either with record players equipped with earphones or in individual listening and viewing booths.

A place should be provided for students to experiment with informal instruments and to record their efforts. Study cubicles for students and preparation centers for teachers are elements of new schools which have merit for certain aspects of the broadened program of education in music.

EQUIPMENT AND SUPPLIES

In addition to pianos and other standard items of equipment, each teaching station should be provided with modern sound reproducing equipment. The music department should

---

[3] *Music Buildings, Rooms, and Equipment.* (Washington: Music Educators National Conference, 1955.)

also have ready access to a wide assortment of teaching aids including tape recorders, projectors, motion picture and film strip projectors, as well as radio and television receivers. Arrangements should make it possible to use these teaching aids in rehearsal rooms as well as in classrooms, in order that the broader objectives of music education may be realized for students in performing groups as well as for those in classroom type instruction.

Autoharps, resonator bells, recorders, and other informal type instruments should be available. Many schools may wish to equip a room for class piano instruction as a way of reaching some of the outcomes.

A diversified collection of recordings, sets of miniature scores, vocal scores, films, and reference books are other important instructional aids that should be provided. Some experimentation has been done in the area of programmed learning in music. These possibilities should also be investigated. The administrator should make every effort to keep up to date on new materials as they become available.

BUDGET

The person responsible for administering the music program will have the task of making specific recommendations regarding the allocation of funds for use in his department and of justifying his recommendations to the superintendent or budget director. An itemized budget request listing specific needs with a brief, appropriate explanation is desirable.

For many schools, the assumption of the task of providing an education in music for all students, rather than only for those who choose to participate in performing organizations, will result in a change in the nature of the budget. The music administrator will need to give careful thought to preparing such an expanded budget. It will be necessary to orient the superintendent's staff and the board of education to this expanded concept of music in general education. The introduction of an expanded music program will involve a fairly large initial investment for equipment items and for library and reference materials that ordinarily might not be provided

BASIC FRAMEWORK FOR A
SIX YEAR HIGH SCHOOL

Grade Level	Basic Requirements of Subject Matter							Requirements at Each Grade Level	Available for Concentration	Reserved for Individual Study	Total Available
	Mathematics	Science	Social Studies	English	Foreign Language	Practical, Visual, and Performing Arts	Physical Education				
7	7	5	5	8	4	8	7	44	10	6	60
8	7	5	5	8	4	6	6	41	11	8	60
9	5	7	5	6	4	5	6	38	12	10	60
10	5	5	5	6	4	5	4	34	16	10	60
11	3	5	5	4	4	3	4	28	20	12	60
12	3	3	5	4	4	3	3	25	21	14	60
Total Minimum Requirements	30	30	30	60		30	30	210	90	60	360
Typical Total Minimum Now	30	20	45	50		20	60	225	135	0	360

Note: All times shown are number of ½ hour periods per week required.

in a conventional program. Once a basic library has been established, it can be adequately maintained with a relatively modest outlay of funds.

Provision should also be made for financing in-service training and the occasional employment of outside consultants. As is pointed out in Chapter VII, those already employed as music teachers in our schools must be helped to prepare themselves to provide education in music for all students if the job is to be accomplished within the next few years. School music budgets might provide tuition aid for teachers to take college workshops. Funds might be allocated for materials and leadership for in-service programs within the school systems. There is much evidence which testifies to the value of in-service training, and school districts large and small are encouraged to provide this type of help for their teachers. Such opportunities should be conceived both in terms of general challenges and inspirations and in terms of specific proposals for content and techniques in teaching.

SCHEDULING

Much experimentation has been going on in the area of scheduling and there is definite evidence to show that the so-called "educational lock-step" of five subjects, five periods per week no longer dominates the high school schedule. The concepts of team teaching, periods of differing length, and flexible class groupings are just a few of the factors that are exerting a decided influence on programming and scheduling.

Quotations from the publication *Focus on Change* indicate the nature of the secondary school schedule of the future:

> Tomorrow's schools will put flexibility of school arrangements ahead of the rigidity of the bell. The day will be divided into 15- or 20-minute modules of time, instead of equal periods, with no standard intermissions when the entire school crowds the halls and rest rooms at once. . . .
>
> Faculty members also will find their day governed by the needs of the curriculum, rather than by the insistence of the bell. Individual teachers will be scheduled 10 to 20 hours per week for class instruction, the number of hours depending upon class purposes and

sizes. The 15- or 20-minute modular arrangement of the school day will allow the flexibility needed to schedule each day according to the nature of the instruction plans.[4]

Possible schedules for the two music instructors in a school using modules of time are shown on pages 170-1. A proposal for organizing the six years of the secondary school is given on page 167.

The role of the principal as the educational leader in developing a practical framework around which a meaningful program can be developed is a pivotal one. The success or failure of a music program is dependent to a large extent on the attitude of the school's administrators and their willingness to organize a schedule that is flexible enough to encompass the diverse requirements of the music program.

STAFF

The ideal facilities, the ultimate in equipment and supplies, the most flexible schedule imaginable are of little or no consequence without a staff of well trained teachers who are equipped musically and intellectually to cope with the heightened demands of a dynamic educational program in music. In many instances the traditionally trained teacher will require a considerable amount of re-orientation. This "re-treading" can take the form of in-service training activities, lectures, demonstrations, or extension courses offered by colleges and universities.

There is a tendency in many high schools to consider vocal and instrumental music as two isolated spheres of interest. Limited contact and lack of communication between teachers are not conducive to the development of a curriculum that takes full advantage of the varied talents of the total staff. Cooperative planning at the school level is essential to an ongoing program that does not overlap and become repetitive. The full utilization of the talents of staff members in other subject areas should not be overlooked.

---

[4] J. Lloyd Trump and Dorsey Baynham, *op. cit.*, pp. 41, 43.

WEEKLY SCHEDULE FOR INSTRUCTOR A

	Monday	Tuesday	*B 3-L A N D	Thursday	Friday
1		2-L		2-L	
2		MUSIC † LIT.		MUSIC LIT.	
3	3-L O		S 3-M T R I		3-L O
4	R		N		R
5	C H .	2-M BAND	G S		C H .
6	3-L B	W. WINDS	B 3-L A		3-L B
7	A N	2-S BEGIN.	N D	2-S BEGIN.	A N
8	D	STRINGS	(FALL)	STRINGS	D
9					
10					
11	2-M MUS. LIT.	I 6-I N	2-M ORCH.	2-M BAND	2-M MUS. LIT.
12	LAB	D I	WINDS	BRASS	LAB
13	2-M BEGIN.	V	2-M MUS. LIT.	2-M BEGIN.	
14	WINDS	I D	LAB	WINDS	
15		N U S A			
16		T L R .			

Large Group...... 16–19 half hour modules
Medium Group ... 19   half hour modules
Small Group...... 4   half hour modules
Individual lessons.. 6   half hour modules

TOTAL...... 45–48 half hour modules

* Special practice for football show part of Fall semester.
† Students in the nonselective music literature class meet twice a week with the whole group and once a week in a smaller laboratory session.

WEEKLY SCHEDULE FOR INSTRUCTOR B

	Monday	Tuesday	Wednesday	Thursday	Friday
1	2-L		2-L		
2	MUSIC † LIT.		MUSIC LIT.		
3			2-L "A"	2-M BOYS	
4	2-L "A"	2-M MUS. LIT.	CHORUS	SECTION.	2-L "A"
5	CHORUS	LAB			CHORUS
6					
7	2-M GIRLS	3-M SELECT CHORUS		3-M SELECT CHORUS	2-M MUS. LIT.
8	CHORUS				LAB
9					
10					
11		2-M BOYS	2-L "B"	2-M MUS. LIT.	I 6-I N
12		SECTION.	CHORUS	LAB	D I
13	2-L "B"	2-S	2-M GIRLS		V I
14	CHORUS	ENSEMBLE	CHORUS		I D N U
15		2-S			S A
16		ENSEMBLE			T L R .

Large Group...... 14 half hour modules
Medium Group ... 20 half hour modules
Small Group...... 4 half hour modules
Individual lessons.. 6 half hour modules

TOTAL...... 44 half hour modules

† Students in the nonselective music literature class meet twice a week with the whole group and once a week in a smaller laboratory session.

LEADERSHIP

In addition to contributing in considerable measure to the areas just described, the director or supervisor of music is charged with the important responsibility of providing guidance and direction to the over-all program of music instruction and seeing that it dovetails with the total educational program. He will make every effort to maintain good rapport with the teaching staff, keeping channels of communication clear and encouraging the free exchange of ideas and expression of opinions.

A junior high school principal has stated the challenge clearly:

> The changes—in curriculum, methodology, technology, school scheduling, and staff development—are more sweeping than the change from sailing ship to steamship, or train to plane. Our passengers are not casual and our freight is precious. The principal who would move to change a school program to prepare for the last third of this century must move boldly yet gently, courageously yet courteously.[5]

[5] Joseph M. Cronin, "The Principal's Role in Change," *The Bulletin* of the National Association of Secondary School Principals, Vol. 47, No. 283 (May 1963), p. 29.

CHAPTER VII

Implications for
Teacher Education

THIS chapter which is devoted to a consideration of the education of the teacher of music in the secondary school should be read in light of the preceding chapters. For the education of the secondary teacher should be closely connected with the accepted aims, objectives, outcomes, and organization of the programs in the secondary schools where he is to teach. It should be emphasized, therefore, that the education (both pre-service and in-service) being advocated for the teacher of music is the type and amount of education deemed to be the most appropriate if the outcomes of Chapter II are to be achieved.

The responsibility for making a musical contribution to general education belongs to the entire school but especially to the music teachers, as was pointed out in Chapter III. *All* music teachers must be proficient in meeting this responsibility.

What, then, should be the appropriate high school and collegiate education of this teacher? How much general education should be provided? How much and what type of work in the field of music? And how much attention should be given to the professional aspect of his program of studies? How many courses? What type? What kinds of experiences with children and with music should be made available to the prospective teacher in preparation for his later responsibilities?

The answers to these questions depend largely on what the prospective secondary school music teacher is later expected to be as he stands in front of a class. They depend also upon what outcomes are accepted as desirable for the program. The reader may at this time wish to review the outcomes of Chapter II, since the recommended education described in the next section of this chapter is predicated upon, and closely tied to, the material in Chapter II.

SUGGESTED PROGRAM OF PREPARATION

Secondary School Level.—Earlier in this chapter a question was asked concerning the appropriate high school education of the music teacher. Because of the broad demands of this teaching field it is felt that a very important part of the education of a teacher with responsibilities for general education in music should take place at the secondary school level. Significant deficiencies at this level will make extremely difficult, if not impossible, the achievement of other purposes and goals usually attached to collegiate education.

For example, it is highly important that at the high school level each prospective teacher of music develop a deep interest in, and an insatiable curiosity about, music. This, of course, might be accomplished in a number of ways, but it seems to depend chiefly upon the student's music teachers at this level—supplemented in many cases by encouragement from home and by opportunity for a breadth of musical experiences, in and out of school.[1]

Next, the prospective teacher of music should, while in high school, develop a reasonable proficiency upon one of the major musical instruments, because desirable proficiency on one or more of these instruments cannot be fully developed during the college years alone.

It should be especially noted that skill on the piano is of importance to all music educators and of particular value to one whose responsibilities are more apt to be broad rather than specialized. Nor should the prospective music teacher neglect the opportunity to learn to use his singing voice while he is in school.

---

[1] See *A Career in Music Education* (Washington, D.C.: Music Educators National Conference, 1962), p. 19.

In addition to a deep and abiding interest in music and a reasonable proficiency on a major musical instrument, the prospective teacher should, while still enrolled in high school, get a good start on his own general education. For, as was described in Chapters I and II, the aims and objectives of music for all students are actually a part of the aims of general education itself. And, if the music teacher himself is not liberally educated, it is not reasonable to assume that he can help his own students later to become more liberally educated through music. Furthermore, this general education cannot be achieved in its fullest sense during the college years unless the work taken at the secondary school level has been chosen wisely and done well. Here reference is made to broad, integrating courses in the natural sciences, the humanities, and the social sciences. High school courses in the social sciences, American, English, and world literature, languages, and in broad aspects of the natural sciences and mathematics should, if taught properly, give this prospective teacher of music a good beginning for his own liberal education. Of course, the student activity program in the secondary school is also quite valuable in developing the depth and breadth of experience necessary for the successful teacher.

Collegiate Level.—As we consider the collegiate level of education, it should be emphasized that these four or five years of post-high-school work are, or should be, merely extensions of what the prospective teacher has already begun at the secondary school level—work in each of the three basic categories mentioned several times above: a) general education; b) specialized work in the field of music (theory, literature, and performance); and c) professional education (that part of the prospective teacher's college education devoted to a consideration of and direct experience with ways in which children and youth can be most effectively helped to learn and profit from content material in a given field of learning).

Of course, most prospective teachers of music will have had, upon entrance to college, varying amounts of work in the first two categories (general education and music), but few if any will have had, prior to college, any contact at all with the third, or professional part of their education. Therefore, the collegiate program must of necessity be designed with enough flexibility to meet the exact needs of each prospective teacher in each of these three categories. Trite as it may be to some educators, it remains imperative that we must "take the students where they are" and move them along as far as we can in the time available.

Proper screening of all applicants for admission to teacher education programs is necessary and is required in Standard III of the National Council for Accreditation of Teacher Education (NCATE). For prospective teachers of music, each institution should apply the criteria it deems appropriate for potential music educators.

This process of screening and selection is a most crucial matter and must be given very careful attention. The quality of the preparation program—however well designed and carried out—would make little difference if no attention were given to the quality and potential of those admitted to the program. For example, those whose deficiencies related to pre-college study are so great as to jeopardize seriously their chances of successfully completing the college program *should,* in most cases, *not be admitted to a preparation program* for music teachers. Disqualifying deficiencies might exist in any of these categories: (a) deep interest in and curiosity about music; (b) reasonable proficiency in piano (or some other major musical instrument) and voice as indicated on page 174; or (c) reasonable depth in general education.

Therefore, any "suggested program of studies" must, if it is to be effective, be flexible enough to allow considerable variation both for the able and ambitious and for those whose experience, achievement, and aptitude are at lower levels on the continuum. This point should be kept in mind as the reader studies the following suggested curriculum.

SUGGESTED FIVE-YEAR CURRICULUM

Semester Hours

I. **General Education** **55**

Humanities (including Fine Arts)   24

Languages and Literature,
including English
Philosophy
Drama and Speech
Architecture
Music in history[2]
Art in history[2]
Others

Social Sciences   15

History
Economics
Citizenship & Government
Sociology
Psychology
Geography
Anthropology
Others

Natural Science & Mathematics   12

Physical Science[3]
Biological Science[3]
Earth Science[3]
History of Science[3]
Chemistry
Physics
Biology
Geology

---

[2] These should not be the traditional "Music History" or "Art History" courses but rather broader courses in general education designed for both the major and non-major in these fields (freshman or sophomore year).

[3] Broad courses, *integrating* several of the more specialized fields of science, are more desirable for general education purposes than narrow, highly specialized courses.

Mathematics
    History of Number Systems[3]
    History of Mathematics[3]
    Fundamental Concepts
      of Mathematics[3]
Physical Education   4

II. **Specialized Work in the Field of Music**....81
    Theory and Composition   18
    Music History and Literature   18
    Performance   27-30
      Piano proficiency required
      Other instruments-ensembles
    Music Education[4]   15-18
      (Would include courses in music
      methods and materials as well as
      a required course giving particu-
      lar attention to and provision for
      achieving the outcomes of music
      in general education.)

III. **Professional Education**[5] 24
    Foundations (Sociological, his-
      torical, and philosophical)   3
    Guidance and Measurement   3
    Human Growth and Development   3
    Learning Theory and the Classroom   3
    Observation of and Participation with
      Children and Youth[6]   3
    Student Teaching   6
    Elective in Professional Education[7]   3

GRAND TOTAL SEMESTER HOURS   **160**

[4]Includes methods and materials in music. See also Professional Education section for additional Music Education.

[5] Other than Music Education.

[6] Since music educators will, in all probability, be called upon to teach music classes other than performing groups, it is recommended that all students have direct experience with such classes.

[7] Could be chosen from audiovisual aids, comparative education, education of the gifted, etc.

The recommendation for a five-year program is in line with a national trend to put all teacher-education pre-service programs on a five-year basis.[8] And particularly for the music educator, who is expected to train and conduct performing groups as well as contribute to the aims of general education, is the five-year program necessary. Any shorter period would result in serious deficiencies in one or more of the three large categories indicated earlier: a) general education; b) concentrated work in music and music education; and c) professional education. It should be made quite clear, however, that a five-year program not only may but probably should be on a "four-plus-one" basis. It should be so designed and offered that a person completing the first four years would be qualified to begin teaching. Then the fifth year could be taken during summers—or in part-time during the year—after some actual teaching experience has been gained. If it is offered on a "four-plus-one" basis, each teacher education institution would revise the five-year program so as to offer the most crucial parts during the first four years.

No amount of course work required of the prospective teacher who is to contribute to general education in music will be effective and really meaningful unless the whole preparation program is accompanied and strongly supported by a positive feeling on the part of the institution involved—and particularly its music and music education faculty—that this phase of music education is important and quite necessary in our public and private schools and that those who teach for these outcomes are just as important in these school systems as any other teachers. Furthermore, these college and university faculty members and administrative officers must be aware that the preparation of these teachers is an extremely important obligation of institutions of higher education. No longer can these institutions and their departments of music be content merely with preparing directors of bands, orchestras, and choruses, and "supervisors of music" for elementary schools. The extent to which colleges and

---

[8] The five-year program may or may not culminate in a master's degree.

universities *and* their music faculties support these premises and take supporting action shall, in large measure, determine whether they do actually graduate persons highly competent to offer a program of music in general education. All future members of the profession of music education should expect to shoulder their responsibility to enhance the general education of pupils through appropriate experiences in and with music.

Getting institutions and their departments of music to take positive and aggressive action about the preparation of teachers with this viewpoint will depend upon many related factors. Various kinds of influence from interested groups can help in this respect. Listed below are some conditions which could help to move an institution toward offering and supporting a sound preparation program for all music educators.

1. Demand on the part of public school principals and superintendents that music teachers be more broadly prepared, in order that they may be able to teach all music classes more effectively, and especially those for non-performing students.[9]

2. Awareness and conviction on the part of college administrators (presidents, deans, department chairmen, etc.) that something must be done about music for *all* children and youth—such awareness and conviction to be followed by more aggressive leadership toward these ends.

3. The realization on the part of many college and university music departments that they will literally go out of existence unless they enlarge their horizons beyond *music performance* as the prime or sole objective of such departments.

4. Communication to college music departments from former graduates now teaching music in junior and senior high schools indicating that the music programs they completed while preparing to teach left much to be desired—

---

[9] Of course, it is recognized that such demands will come only if and when these public school administrators are much more aware of the need for more attention to musical outcomes for all students.

especially in connection with the possibilities of music for every child.

5. Requirements by certifying and accrediting agencies that adequate attention to the general education responsibilities of music teachers be included in *all* preparation programs of prospective music teachers.

It should be repeated here that the authors of this publication of the Music Educators National Conference recommend that all music teachers—present and future—work to be men and women who are well educated in the broadest sense. All must be sound musicians. Those who choose to work with the musically talented students found in secondary school performing groups must be willing and eager, as well as able, to lead their pupils to the broad outcomes listed in Chapter II, in conjunction with their combined efforts to polish their performance skills. The teachers who choose to bring music to the other students in the school must be considered no less important and must be no less competent musicians. They must, in addition, possess great teaching skill, a deep liking for and understanding of youth, and a broad knowledge of music in order to be successful with those who may be less motivated toward musical scholarship and performance.

In-Service Education

All programs described thus far have been for the *prospective teacher*—the *pre-service* part of the teacher's education. Equally as important, however, is the *in-service* program—help and support for those teachers already in the field. In fact, this in-service group is, in terms of time, far more important than the pre-service group, if we expect actually to make material progress with the musical outcomes in our secondary schools within the next few years. For, even if *all* persons graduating from teacher education programs in music during the next decade were prepared in this phase of music education as well as in other forms, we would not have nearly enough teachers for our schools to provide the broad program of music education that is recommended here. It is imperative, therefore, that we consider ways in which this in-service group can be helped to carry on music classes more effectively. Listed below are some suggestions relating to this group.

1. Colleges and universities could organize, publicize, and offer workshops for in-service music teachers. The workshops, obviously, must be organized to meet the particular needs of the in-service music teachers. Some will want to broaden their contact with music literature or to extend their study of music theory. Opportunities for increased liberal education, or professional training that would enable the teachers to use their musical skills and knowledges more effectively for general education purposes, will be needed by others. Formal organization and credit must be of less concern than offering assistance that will result in better teachers of music for general education purposes. The workshops may be offered for credit, however, and could be held at any of several times: (a) in concentrated periods (two or three weeks) during the summer; or (b) on several successive Saturdays during the fall or spring; or (c) in late afternoons or early evenings during a part of the school year; or (d) at other times which would suit the particular group being served.

2. School systems could, as a part of their own in-service program, organize workshops in music for their music teachers. Such workshops might be cooperatively developed by two or more systems, in conjunction with some nearby college or university, and they might be held either at one of the junior or senior high schools or on the college campus. These would usually be held in late afternoons (perhaps one afternoon a week for a semester) or on Saturdays.

3. Increasing attention could be given to music in general education at professional meetings, particularly those of the MENC federated state units.

4. Colleges, universities, and state departments of education could develop and distribute materials specifically designed to improve the program of music in general education.

5. Colleges and universities could, in cooperation with public or private school administrators and music teachers,

set up pilot programs in one or more junior or senior high schools. Such programs should be described and evaluated for others who might wish to start similar ones.

In summary, the reader's attention is called particularly to the following points:

• The teacher who, through music, is to enhance the general education of the children and youth with whom he works must first of all be a liberally educated person himself.

• The preparation of this teacher must be properly balanced among its three main components: general education, specialized work in music, and professional education. None of these three should be omitted or considered unimportant.

• The full education of the teacher described in this chapter includes experiences in elementary school, high school, *and* institutions of higher education.

• Screening and selection of prospective teachers of music are most critical and at the same time are perhaps the most neglected factors in this whole matter.

• The college preparation of this teacher we need and hope for should be at least five years in length, but preferably on a "four-plus-one" basis.

• Most critical is the attitude of departments of music and administrators in institutions of higher education toward the role of the teacher who, through music, is expected to help improve the general education level of all students in elementary and secondary schools. A positive and favorable attitude is not only desirable. It is imperative.

• Improvement is mandatory in the pre-service and in-service programs for the development of the teacher needed to help children and youth accomplish these broader aims of music education.

• Each person reading this book could exercise a favorable and positive influence in helping to achieve the objectives and goals outlined in this and preceding chapters. These things will be accomplished only if many individuals and groups work together effectively.

CHAPTER VIII

Promising Practices

IN the course of the several years that this project has been under way, the members of the committee have encountered evidence that many individual music educators are solving the problems of general education in music in a variety of ways. Since imaginative teaching is what is needed most in this area, and since accounts of such solutions may better spark the thinking of other teachers than all the lists of experiences and materials, a good deal of space will be devoted to descriptions of music teaching that serves general education objectives. It is suggested that readers refrain from writing the individuals or school systems mentioned for further information. Most of them will not have material for distribution nor time for extensive correspondence.

Uniformity of presentation of this material will not be possible since it comes from many sources—magazine articles, official reports, programs, instructional materials, and forms filled out for this project. It is hoped that its inclusion here will prove helpful.

CASE STUDY ILLUSTRATIONS

A high school band uses a competition piece as a starting point for studying the Late Baroque era.

Our high school band has just finished a project which came about as a center of interest project during the second semester of the school year. We planned to play the Bach-Moehlmann *Prelude and Fugue in D Minor* for district competition. The students showed a growing interest in polyphonic music which led to an interesting study of the Baroque period. We listened to a recording of E. Power Biggs playing the original composition from the *Eight Little Preludes and Fugues* for organ. The organ on which Biggs played was an organ Bach had played during his lifetime. Instruments of the Baroque period were discussed and several recorders were played before the class. Characteristics of the music and art of the period were discussed which led to a collection of reproductions of Baroque paintings and pictures of architecture for the bulletin board. Other composers and their contemporary writers of literature and poetry were discussed along with painters of the period.

A visit to hear the Bach Festival at Rollins College was arranged and attended by a great number of the band members. The students saw and heard a real harpsichord for the first time. The study of the Baroque was culminated with a church concert in our school community which featured music of the period. The program included music of Purcell, Buxtehude, Bach, Handel, and Marcello. The high school glee club presented vocal numbers along with the instrumental music. Several brass ensemble numbers with organ and Bach organ solos were played by teacher and students. This church concert was one of the musical high points of the year for both the community and the music department of the school.

Through this study our band not only had a better appreciation for the period, its composers and their music, but it was able to present the composition for the district contest with some feeling for the interpretation of the style which was required for a superior performance.

The teaching of general music in band, directed toward the humanities and music's relationship to the other arts, has given band a new perspective in our school. Other teachers are looking on our work as being worthwhile for they can see results that carry over into their classes. For instance, students choose to write about composers and arts in their English composition classes. . . . We must give the students all that we are able and trained to give them. A broader band program can be the answer.

CRESCENT CITY (FLORIDA) HIGH SCHOOL
Charles Ruhl, *Band Director*

Planned assembly programs, utilizing professional symphony players, provide music education for all students.

The Greenhills-Forest Park City Schools outside Cincinnati have developed musical assembly programs in addition to the regular music classes. These assemblies are designed to provide experience in the chronological and stylistic development of the humanities.

In cooperation with the Cincinnati Musicians Association (AF of M Local #1) and the Music Performance Trust Fund of the Recording Industries, string quartets, woodwind and brass ensembles composed of members of the Cincinnati Symphony Orchestra are brought to each school to perform for student assemblies. Explanations, demonstrations, and performances are made under the direction of the schools' director of music, James Riley, who *teaches* rather than entertains the children. The ensembles are presented throughout one school year. The following two years are devoted to similar programs presented by the Cincinnati Little Symphony Orchestra, a chamber orchestra made up of the first-desk players of the Cincinnati Symphony. Riley arranges the programs, conducts, and provides the commentary for the children. The programs are presented in school time. The three year cycle provides the opportunity to concentrate first on the instrument families and then on symphonic programs which are related to art, literature, and social studies.

Classroom teachers meet with music specialists to discuss and select areas to be covered during the year. Program material is provided for the elementary teachers to help in the preparation for the assemblies. Music supervisors assist in this preparation in the various buildings to which they are assigned. All of this is in addition to the other aspects of the music program which includes singing, reading, and listening.

A typical program might be devoted to the music of a particular composer. Another might correlate art and music using illustrations to make a stylistic comparison between painting, architecture, and music. Still another might be based on the music of France and employ the elementary French classes for singing and dancing.

Results are reported in carry-over to art, history, English, and foreign language classes. Performing groups benefit and demonstrate their enlarged understanding through more intelligent performances of various musical styles. A tangible result is the string program which has developed an orchestra that received a superior rating at the state festival of the Ohio Music Educators Association. The entire music program is aided, and intelligent and sympathetic listeners are added to the student body and the community. The program, initiated in 1959, has continued to expand with the growth of this suburban school system.

GREENHILLS-FOREST PARK
(OHIO) CITY SCHOOLS
James Riley, *Director of Music*

Six teachers form a team for a humanities program.

Two music teachers, two art teachers, a drama coach, and a teacher of history work together as a team in a unified learning experience that does not involve organizing a new course.

They have developed one-hour presentations around each of the several stylistic periods (Renaissance, Baroque, Classical, etc.). During a given day the six teachers spend all six periods together as a team. The students who would normally come to them in their individual rooms, on this day report to a large assembly room. There they are introduced to a stylistic period by the whole team. With the Renaissance presentation, for example, the history teacher opened the session with a short talk which described what was going on in Italy in the 16th century. A short film on the Renaissance was shown. The art teachers made presentations on Leonardo da Vinci and Michelangelo. The drama teacher discussed the work and times of Shakespeare. The music teachers illustrated their discussion with recordings of Renaissance music.

The several presentations were spaced at intervals of approximately six weeks. During the course of the year 1200 students who are in the classes of these six teachers were provided with an integrated introduction to the humanities. No special programing or course organization was required. Considerable interest in the approach developed on the part of the entire school and in the community. The six teachers presented a demonstration lesson to the faculty and the board of education.

LIVERMORE SENIOR HIGH SCHOOL
LIVERMORE, CALIFORNIA
Gerald Stasko ⎫
Owen Goldsmith ⎬ *music teachers*

A unified humanities class relates music to man and to the other arts.

Fairview High School inaugurated a required program dealing with basic concepts for living for all students throughout the school. *Freshmen* concentrate their thinking on that area concerned with adjustment to high school studying and living. *Sophomores* are concerned with the more objective areas of science and mathematics. The *Junior* class pointed its attention to the backgrounds of American Democracy. The *Senior* class delved into the deeper meaning of the Humanities. We are here concerned only with the senior portion—the Humanities.

As a basis for this course, each student was asked to draw upon all of his individual life experiences for various points of reference. There was no basic text other than the individual's own life.

As motivational material, the guide for the course was basically a much expanded presentation of the Encyclopaedia Britannica films on the HUMANITIES which deal with the various aspects of man's search for truth as seen through three dramas: Thornton Wilder's *Our Town*, Sophocles' *Oedipus Rex*, and Shakespeare's *Hamlet*. With these twelve films magnificently presented in color and dramatized by the Stratford-on-Avon players of Ontario, Canada, the class witnessed the passing of history and the interrelation of the arts: art, architecture, drama, music, the dance, language and custom as they relate themselves to mankind.

The senior class of some 350 students met for one (1) fifty-minute period each week in the school auditorium. Materials were then selected and discussed in individual classes of advanced literature, language, and social problems classes following the mass lecture. Guest lecturers were brought in to augment the presentations of the school faculty. Dr. Henry C. Montgomery of Miami University spoke on the Greek theater. Dr. Richard Baker of the University of Dayton gave a concise presentation of the Greek mind and spirit. The Miami University Oxford String Quartet and Mrs. Dulcie Demette Barlow of Richmond, Indiana presented a musical program representing the music of the Baroque, Classic, Romantic, and Contemporary periods of writing. Mrs. Grace Wolff and Mr. Michael Solomon of the Dayton Bureau of Recreation and Parks presented a folk dance demonstration using students from the class to illustrate the folk expression of South America and Europe, and included in their presentation folk games and customs.

As further illustration of the dance as an art form expression, the film of the Martha Graham dance troupe presenting the Aaron Copland ballet *Appalachian Spring* was presented and discussed.

A panel of local clergy presented a stimulating discussion of the concept of God and man, and man's idea of himself and his religion. This was a culminating panel following the presentation of the Sophocles drama. Following the panel, those students so desiring retired to a discussion area to query the clergy further. This was a highlight of the series.

Other film presentations included: Walt Disney's *Toot, Whistle, Plunk and Boom,* and *Donald in Math-Magic Land.*

Recordings and musical examples were employed in context whenever it was necessary to illustrate a musical term or for clarification of material.

Students kept notebooks for their own information and future reference. Periodically, students were given quizzes covering the presented material. Notebooks were collected and checked at intervals.

Each of the music sessions began with group singing either by rote from the folk song repertoire or from the vast collection of carol settings. The songs were then used as illustrative material to explain the meaning of monophony, polyphony, texture, structure, round, ground bass, canon, ostinato, etc. Rhythmic combinations were presented and clapped en masse. Recorded compositions were chosen to further illustrate these basic concepts; that is—for example, the canon, the theme and variations as found in the Copland ballet *Appalachian Spring*. The students had seen the film, heard the music, and identified the Shaker tune. Students commented on the value of such common experience in understanding the explanations.

The architecture discussion centered around a presentation of color slides representing those various ways man has chosen to build shelter for himself and his family across the globe and through the ages.

Students felt a need for a question and answer period immediately following each general presentation. In the original proposed plan, it was hoped that material first presented in the master lecture would be further explained by the individual subject teachers, a procedure which met with varied degrees of success in actual practice.

The majority of seniors advised that the program be further developed and expanded. Seeing the arts as the record of man's thought, they felt, gave them an opportunity to organize their thinking and to gain confidence in expressing their most basic feelings through the humanities.

FAIRVIEW HIGH SCHOOL
DAYTON, OHIO
George H. Zimmerman, *Music Consultant*
Dorothy Herbst, *Humanities Coordinator*
Theresa Folger, *Principal*

A junior high school music teacher who has succeeded in making his music classes more of an academic discipline, prepares tapes for the use of other teachers in his system.

Tapes investigating five questions—"What is music?" "What is rhythm?" "What is melody?" "What is harmony?" "What is form?"—were prepared to serve as a point of reference around which five entire units of study might be developed. The tapes are used in different ways by teachers who are thus able to keep their teaching creative. A teacher's guide, student study sheets, and a list of recordings of major works on the tapes are provided.

These tapes function at two distinct levels. First, they serve to introduce the student to a great variety of musical ideas arranged in an easy to follow sequence that is easily remembered. These points of musical interest are made in simple language but each idea about music is chosen for its ability to be greatly expanded by the classroom teacher. The comments on the tapes are intended as a creative outline containing an exciting outline of ideas about music, illustrated with numerous musical examples, which the creative classroom teacher can enlarge in many different directions depending on his or her background and interests. Second, it was the belief of the author that students must describe musical works to understand them, and these taped examples serve as excellent exercises in describing many different musical styles and learning to identify music by its texture, sound, treatment of melody, and form. Some of the tapes contain over sixty musical examples.

PLAN A.—1. Read the teacher study guide carefully.
2. Organize all materials that you wish to add to the outline.
3. Listen to the tape in question three times. During each hearing concentrate on *one* of the two areas listed below:
1st hearing: General plan of the tape. Points on which you will enlarge.
2nd hearing: Points to be made from the examples. Record the footage of examples to which you plan to return in your discussion of the material.

4. Play the tape for the class. After the first hearing, review basic points and answer questions. Try to stimulate the imagination and create an attitude of academic adventure which will stay with the class until you meet with them again.

5. Begin the next class with a discussion of the things that the students remember from the tape.

6. Go from a mastery of the materials on the tape into your enlargement of the topic area. One tape could easily serve as the basis for a semester's work, but it need not occupy you for a longer period of time than you deem necessary.

7. Play complete recording of some of the examples used.

PLAN B.—1. Read the teacher study guide carefully.

2. Listen to the tapes.

3. Outline your entire unit of study.

4. Present the tape to the class without any discussion before the first hearing.

5. In the second session hear just one half of the tape and define all words that may be a problem. Answer questions brought up by class.

6. In the next session hear the second half of the tape and follow the same procedure (as in #5).

7. Play the tape in smaller units for mastery of all outline points.

8. Go on into your larger unit of study and refer to the tape for reinforcement.

9. Play complete recording of some of the examples used.

Note to the teacher:

Try to develop a plan within your school whereby interested pupils may be able to listen to recordings of the musical examples. Also encourage out-of-school listening, at home or at such places as the music department of the Logan Square Library.

The tapes provide in one convenient package many unusual sounds not readily available to classroom teachers, as well as excerpts from larger works used for illustration. Teachers are encouraged to develop a plan whereby pupils may be able to listen to these compositions in their entirety and to build their own record libraries.

PHILADELPHIA PUBLIC SCHOOLS
E. Page Bailey

Cooperative assemblies (music, physical education, English, and art) demonstrate the "universality of music" to the entire student body of a junior high school.

McMillan Junior High School in Omaha, Nebraska, has been the site of an experiment in bringing music to all the students of the school, an effort involving the cooperation and active participation of every faculty member and administrator.

John Q. Adams, director of instrumental music at McMillan, believed that music could be a unifying and integrating force in the whole school curriculum. He was able to convince his colleagues that music could show every student, regardless of his abilities, the way to an appreciation of the fine arts and an understanding of the relationships among all the areas of the curriculum. The faculty agreed to try out a conception of the assembly as an integral curriculum unit for the whole school.

For the first experiments, the departments of English, art, and physical education—each of which has a unique relationship to music—were selected to work with the music department. Each assembly program was carefully planned to fit the mental, physical, and emotional needs and capacities of the teen-agers who were the audience and performers. These were not "fun" assemblies calculated to fill time and entertain by appealing to undeveloped tastes. They were learning experiences made enjoyable through an imaginative presentation and a thorough understanding of the needs of the audience.

While each program was in preparation, preliminary study material, together with suggestions for its use, was distributed to the school, and the faculty's cooperation in carrying through these suggestions contributed largely to the success of the assemblies.

Descriptions of several programs will best illustrate the variety of subjects covered and the nature of their treatment.

A program on "American Dance from the Minuet to *My Fair Lady*" was prepared cooperatively by the music and physical education departments. The senior orchestra played while the girls' physical education classes arranged and performed the dances. The participation of such a large group served to heighten the interest. Study materials distributed to all classes prepared the whole student body to enjoy the performance intelligently. Program notes reinforced the information studied beforehand.

Several programs were concerned with coordinating music and creative writing. Students from the ninth grade English class attended an orchestra rehearsal and subsequently wrote descriptive essays or vignettes about what the music suggested to them. These efforts were read before an assembly after the orchestra performed the selections they had been rehearsing.

In another program titled "Impressions," students from the art department came before the audience to paint or sketch their impressions of the music the orchestra was playing. In preparation for this program, it was suggested that students in other classes try their hand at such an activity while listening to recorded music. Both the creative writing and the "Impressions" programs emphasized the variety of individual responses possible to the same musical composition.

Still another program attempted to draw parallels between the stylistic characteristics of the music and art of the Renaissance, Baroque, Classical, Romantic, Impressionistic, and Modern periods. Program notes described the styles both of music and art, listed a few names of composers and artists from each period, and explained the specific choral or instrumental selection performed as an example of a style. Suggestions were made to teachers that they prepare students by spending a little time viewing and discussing representative works of art and becoming familiar, at least by name, with some of the great musicians and artists of history.

The assembly program has been operative in McMillan Junior High School since 1959. In appraising its success, John Adams says:

"We are happy with the outcome of this program. The students enjoy the assemblies, look forward to them, and, most important, they learn and retain what they have learned. The faculty are in general agreement that these programs have been a valuable addition to our curriculum.

"We encountered little difficulty in incorporating the time for the assemblies into the schedule. Our administration was understandably pleased at the prospect of making the undeniably expensive music equipment work for the whole school. Once everyone was convinced that this was an educative project and not merely entertainment, it was relatively easy to overcome scheduling problems.

"There is room for further expansion and improvement. Most of the content of general music classes could be presented in programs of this nature. Programs could be planned around music and musical instruments from other cultures, or a comparison of music from primitive cultures now existing, or the development of American jazz and its influence on the American culture (and vice versa), or an explanation of the physical nature of music, etc.

"We feel that the plan is flexible enough to be usable in almost any school with a forward-looking administrator, a cooperative faculty, and musical leadership. More cooperation between all the departments of a school, more integration of the subject matter of the various courses, is necessary now if we are to produce individuals capable of understanding and dealing with a very complicated world. Music can be a powerful force toward such integration, if we use it properly."

> McMillan Junior High School
> Omaha, Nebraska
> John Q. Adams, *Director of Instrumental Music*

A junior high school has succeeded in creating a healthy atmosphere for learning in music.

Building on a strong elementary music program that starts in the kindergarten, John Jay High School offers required music courses of substance in the seventh and eighth grades.

When students enter the seventh grade they already know musical notation and can use it to take dictation. They have learned to listen to music and have had the opportunity to play instruments and sing in choirs.

Students in the seventh and eighth grades devote three class periods a week to the study of music history, current events, musical form, and directed learning. Two other periods are spent in choir in which the study of music literature is the major concern. Pupils regard the arts as an integral part of their education and they learn to interpret great thoughts and ideas of the past and present. They understand that music reflects periods and that creative minds are to be admired and cherished. Failing in music is considered as unfavorably by the student body as failure in any other subject.

As evidence of the success of this program, elective music in grades 9-12 involves over 50% of the students in performing groups and a school of less than 500 pupils is able to offer a major in music with the following sequence of courses: Music Literature and Materials, Counterpoint, Harmony, and Advanced Harmony.

JOHN JAY HIGH SCHOOL
KATONAH, NEW YORK
Sonia L. Lanman, *Head of the Music Department*

The entire high school student body meets together for music experiences.

With limited faculty and facilities and a school board that feels that everyone should be exposed to music, Orleans High School has scheduled the whole school together for two music lessons a month. One of these is devoted to listening experience and music films while the other is given over to general assembly singing. While the staff holds no illusions about this being a satisfactory program for general education in music, it does represent an attempt to do something for all students rather than complete abdication in the face of difficulty.

ORLEANS (VERMONT) HIGH SCHOOL
James Hayford, *Music Teacher*

An instrumental teacher studies musical periods with his band and orchestra and shares the experience with the school.

Band and orchestra periods in this school give attention to musical content as well as to performance. Both groups are studying styles of the various musical periods. The instructor has worked out informational material on the Baroque, Classical, Romantic, and Contemporary periods. Students are expected to read these study sheets outside class and short tests are given from time to time. During the time that a given period is being studied, representative selections are rehearsed. At the conclusion of the unit of study, a concert is presented in the school cafeteria (no auditorium is available) which seats approximately 250 persons. Teachers who wish to bring their classes to the concerts sign up in advance and the concerts are given during the period in which the performing group regularly rehearses—orchestra, 1st period; band, 2nd period. Each concert is given to a capacity audience. Program notes are handed to each member of the audience and the programs are built around the music of the period currently being studied.

In addition to the emphasis upon musical style, about five minutes at the beginning of each rehearsal are spent in having students of both band and orchestra do vocal sight reading. Melodies from folk and composed literature, in various keys and clefs are in the rehearsal folders in dittoed form. As the students sing, they are taught something about keys, chord feeling, and melodic construction.

The performance level of these groups has not suffered in the least and they both received top superior ratings in the spring festivals. One of the orchestral adjudicators said that the orchestra was the finest high school orchestra he had ever heard. He was particularly impressed with the fidelity of its performance to the classical tradition.

Evaluation in these classes is based upon not only perform-ance, but also upon tests, outside reading, and understand-ing of music theory.

EL CERRITO HIGH SCHOOL
RICHMOND, CALIFORNIA
Marvin Nelson, *Band and Orchestra Director*

Fine arts study is required for high school graduation.

Requirements for graduation from Los Angeles city senior high schools now include one semester of study in the fine arts. This requirement may be met by the completion of a course in either art or music. It has been pointed out that "the emphasis is upon the arts as a part of general education rather than upon specialized activities. In music, courses which fulfill the requirement may involve performance, but they must include such intellectually oriented activities as directed listening, reading, and discussion which will lead to an understanding of the inherent nature and function of music as an art."[1]

The subject matter recommended for study has been or-ganized conceptually. A concept is a mental image that re-mains in the mind after a perceptual experience. No individ-ual can give another a concept. Each person must develop his own. In its beginning stages, a concept may be merely a general notion. As it becomes more and more clarified, it will also become more specific. The first step in conceptual development is perception. In the case of music, this re-quires listening. A performer may be producing a phrase through his own physical activity, but he will not perceive the music until the sound of it has penetrated not only his ears, but also his mind. The development of tonal concepts

---

[1] *Junior and Senior High School Graduation Requirements and Curricula,* 1961 Revision. (Los Angeles City Schools: Division of Instructional Services, Publication No. r89), p. 17.

—the ability to remember, think, and image tone—is essential to musical growth. Musical experiences of young people are therefore truly educative to the degree that they contribute to the ability to think musically, to hear tone in the mind when no sound is made.

LOS ANGELES PUBLIC HIGH SCHOOLS
William C. Hartshorn, *Supervisor in Charge, Music Education*

Students in chorus, band, or orchestra also enroll in classes in theory, history, appreciation, and conducting.

A four-course music cycle was organized at Elizabethtown, Kentucky to provide students with a well-rounded musical education, rather than four years of rehearsal sessions. Students scheduled a performance group and the music course being offered that year, and received ½ credit for each. For nine weeks the rehearsals were held three days a week (MWF) and the class sessions two (TTh). The pattern was reversed at the end of that period so that each activity averaged 2½ periods per week throughout the year. By correlating the material covered in class and rehearsals and by limiting the amount of outside class performance the performance level of the organizations does not suffer from the loss of one half the rehearsal time but can even be raised. Students play and sing better because they understand what they are doing and why they are doing it.[2]

Kenneth L. Neidig

A course for high school seniors relates English, art, and music.

The Art-English-Music Seminar as taught in the high schools of Arlington County (Virginia) Public Schools is a single course embracing the three disciplines. It is open to

---

[2] For a more complete discussion of this program see Kenneth L. Neidig, "An Opera That Just Happened," *Music Educators Journal*, 49 (November-December, 1962), p. 49.

seniors who have a grade of C or above in English in both the tenth and eleventh grades and who have a genuine interest in developing their knowledge of the arts. Classes are held to a maximum of twenty-five students. The students receive two credits for the completion of the Seminar, one in English, and one-half each in art and music.

The actual division of time into units of instruction in the Art-English-Music Seminar is kept flexible to enable the addition of cultural opportunities as they become available in the community. It may be planned so that English is taught at one period and art and music alternate on the other. It may also be taught in blocks of two periods a day with English being taught for two days, art one day, and music one day. One day a week, usually Friday, is frequently used for seminars and field trips. Field trips may be held at the individual school for the local student group, or students may be transported to one of the participating schools for demonstrations or lectures, or the entire group of Seminar students may attend an event or visit an art gallery as a field trip experience.

These Seminar laboratory experiences may consist of a survey of all the arts offered in the Washington, D. C. area. These include drawing, painting, industrial design, ballet, dance, opera, concerts, recitals, dramatics, poetry, or creative writing. Field trips have included Arena Stage play rehearsals, Washington Opera Society opera rehearsals, ballet, performances, and architecture-travel-lectures. Home field trips have included modern dance demonstrations, ballet demonstration-lectures, lectures by modern artists, poetry reading, and a demonstration-lecture by a collector of unusual musical instruments. Two recitals were given by the music teachers, one a vocal recital and the other a harpsichord-piano demonstration-lecture. Field trips on school time are a required part of the course. Evening field trips are optional because of the involvement of fees for tickets.

The philosophy underlying the English-Art-Music Seminar is that literature, art, and music are an expression of life in terms of truth and beauty. It is the aim in the English-Art-Music Seminar to recognize the universal qualities which make creations in the three areas of art an ageless part of our heritage. Since the Seminar offers the twelfth grade English credit necessary for graduation, a study of great literary works is the focus of the course. A recognition of similiar contrasting themes and moods expressed in art and music serve to strengthen the students' recognition of these universal humanistic themes, as developed in the English class. The seminar approach is used in teaching this course. Discussion and research aid the students in relating abstract ideas to their own experiences.

The benefits of this course are both tangible and intangible. It is not possible to measure the cultural growth of students who for the first time in their lives attend an opera, go to a ballet, hear an artist describe his works, attend the rehearsal of a professionally-produced play. They begin to have doors opened for them, to feel at home with the arts. It is possible to observe development in maturity and poise in students, to watch them learn how to become more comfortable and more skilled as participants in seminar discussions, and to observe their increased ability at abstract thinking.

ARLINGTON (VIRGINIA) PUBLIC SCHOOLS
Florence Booker, *Supervisor of Vocal Music*
Richard E. Wiggin, *Supervisor of Art Education*
Fred Carpenter, *Supervisor of English*

A university laboratory school reports on the first ten years of its program of instrumental music for all students.

All students at the University School of Florida State University study instrumental music. After many opportunities to see and hear the instruments in the first four grades every fifth grade student participates in an exploratory instrumental program. The program is designed to help each child discover the band or orchestral instrument for which he is best suited. After a week of demonstrations and instruction on assembling and caring for the instruments, each child lists, in order of preference, three instruments he wishes to play— a string, and two others. He is then given approximately seven weeks instruction on his first choice. Each fifth grade class of thirty students has instrumental music as a class which meets on alternate days with other classroom activities. During the next six weeks students receive instruction on their second choice and then six weeks are devoted to his third choice. At the end of this exploratory program each student makes his final choice of instrument. Instruction continues on the same every other day schedule for the remainder of the year and through the sixth grade. Instrumental music as part of the general education curriculum is continued in the seventh and eighth grades of the University School.

During the 1963-1964 school year 72 percent of those enrolled in the high school division of the University School elected to be members of the performing musical organizations. Of the students who have been in the program since the fifth grade, 85 percent elected music courses in high school and 95 percent indicated they attended concerts regularly.[3]

FLORIDA STATE UNIVERSITY
Glenn Frederick Heinlein, *Associate Professor of Education*

A community formulates a cultural development curriculum with emphasis on the elementary schools.

Concerned over the fact that music class experiences had been reduced to a community sing type of activity by the pressure of increased enrollments, Westmont, Illinois experimented with a program designed to inculcate cultural values. The most unusual facet of the program is the humanities approach at the primary level, beginning with the first grade. The study of music as a discipline is also introduced at this

---

[3] For a more complete description of this program see Glenn Frederick Heinlen, "Instrumental Music in General Education," *Music Educators Journal*, 51 (April-May, 1965), p. 54.

level, involving its own inquiry, skills, activities, along with those of art and poetry. Members of the choir analyze and study the history, period, style, of all choral music sung. Music classes also focus attention on the background of the music studied, sung, and played. Students relate the music to other creative arts. The fundamental elements of music, art, and literature are analyzed.

This campaign for culture was waged on three fronts: (a) teacher education through in-service programs in art and music, teacher presence in class during demonstration classes, involvement in the actual teaching of the arts, attendance at concerts, assemblies, and discussion groups at school; (b) parent education through bulletins, PTA talks, demonstrations, attendance at concert assemblies at school, influence from children who have research projects and assignments involving listening to radio, TV, and phonograph; (c) education of the children through related study of the arts in class, cultural assemblies, art shows, concerts, and films. Concerts by eminent artists are becoming the rule rather than the exception, and the creative arts are an integral part of the entire curriculum.

The whole town having become involved, the reputation of the program has spread and visiting teachers and administrators join in art and music workshops.

WESTMONT (ILLINOIS) PUBLIC SCHOOLS
Donald Elbert, *Superintendent*
Rodney Borstad, *Director of Curriculum*
Georgiana Peterson, *Music Coordinator*

An art teacher and a music teacher present a class together.

In the eleventh and twelfth grades, students in Mansfield, Ohio were provided the opportunity to view and study the various periods and types of the fine arts (painting, sculpture, architecture) and to listen to and study the various periods and types of music. Guest lecturers were brought into the classroom or the class was taken on field trips to concerts or art shows. Students were required to attend at least three concerts and three art shows during the course of this full year offering in addition to the field trips. The class met five days a week and students received one credit for the year's work. After two years of teaching the combined course, the instructors felt that it would be better to teach music for one semester and art for another, rather than attempt the combination.

MANSFIELD, OHIO
Mary Jane Bolus, *Art Teacher*
Norman Gaines, *Music Teacher*
Robert Glass, *Principal*

A junior high school uses music for a school-wide opening exercise.

North Junior High School in West Chester, Pennsylvania, has recently revised its opening exercises to correlate with the morning homeroom period. To establish the proper atmosphere, short musical selections (approximately three minutes in duration) are played over the public address system. These are selected by the music teacher. Following this musical prelude, appropriate thoughts for the day are read by a student. These prose or poetry selections are chosen by members of the English department. The public address system is then silent to permit the salute to the flag in individual homerooms. Notices and announcements are then read over the system and the homeroom period is terminated.

Student comments such as "repeat the selection you played this morning" or "can we hear the rest of it?" indicate that pupils who are otherwise not exposed to music are being made aware of the art and its effects.

NORTH JUNIOR HIGH SCHOOL
WEST CHESTER, PENNSYLVANIA
Ruth Naylor Shaffer, *Music Teacher*

CHAPTER IX

Recapitulation

This book challenges all music educators to return to their original role—to accept as their first responsibility the time-honored objective of music for every child.

Music education was general education in the public schools of nineteenth century America. It has remained a part of the general education of today's elementary schools—those schools that approximate the "common" schooling of the nineteenth century. As secondary education became part of the "common" schooling, music education was allowed to become a special subject and many music educators today are concerned with only a small percentage of the student body. This is an abdication of the profession's original charge.

In making this challenge, the authors advance ideas that could bring about some major revisions in the pattern of music education in this country. Chief among them are the following:

• General education in music must be planned over the entire 12 or 13 years of a student's school life and should not be limited to the elementary years plus a course or two in junior high school.

• Every school system needs to (a) develop well-defined goals for music in general education, (b) plan a twelve-year curriculum to achieve these goals, and (c) systematically evaluate the results.

• All music educators must come to recognize the general education nature of school music experiences and to place this aspect of their teaching before activities which promote vocational skills, entertainment, or school public relations.

• Musical learnings are the responsibility of the entire school—the principal, all the faculty, the students themselves, as well as the music educators.

• Musical performing organizations should exist as laboratory groups to provide educational experiences for their members and for the school as a whole.

• The secondary school music teacher who directs performing groups has the responsibility of organizing his rehearsals in a way which will permit his pupils to improve not only their technical skills but to grow also in their understandings of, and attitudes toward, music as an art.

• A thorough rethinking of secondary school music offerings will undoubtedly result in new scheduling practices which may well mean the abandonment of daily single period rehearsals for large groups.

• The relationship between music at school and music at home needs to be strengthened; schools can assist pupils and parents in finding satisfactory musical experiences that fit the family situation.

• An extensive in-service training program is needed to re-orient thinking with respect to the objectives of secondary school music experiences, and to assist those teachers whose training has been primarily performance oriented toward a more thorough understanding of the structure and literature of music.

• A five-year collegiate program for prospective music educators is necessary to provide the breadth of education needed to meet these challenges adequately.

• All future members of the profession of music education should expect to assume their responsibility to enhance the general education of pupils through appropriate experiences in and with music.

Bibliography

American Council of Learned Societies. "Report of the Music Panel," *ACLS Newsletter*, IX, No. 9 (November, 1958).

Anderson, Donald. "Survey of Musical Style for Band," *Missouri Journal of Research in Music Education*, I (Autumn, 1962), 41-45. (Also published in Hoffer, *Teaching Music in the Secondary Schools*.)

Andrews, Frances, and Joseph Leeder. *Guiding Junior High School Pupils in Music Experiences*. Englewood Cliffs, New Jersey: Prentice-Hall, Inc., 1953.

Apel, Willi. *Harvard Dictionary of Music*. Cambridge, Massachusetts: Harvard University Press, 1944.

Aristotle. "Politics," Book VIII of *The Basic Works of Aristotle*. Translated by B. Jewett. New York: Random House, 1941.

Art and Music. *Educational Media Index 3*. New York: McGraw-Hill Book Co., Inc., 1964.

Baines, Anthony. *Woodwind Instruments and Their History*. Revised edition. New York: W. W. Norton & Co., Inc., 1963.

Baines, Anthony. *Musical Instruments Through the Ages*. Baltimore: Penguin Books, Inc., 1961.

Baker, Theodore. *Bakers Biographical Dictionary of Musicians*. 5th edition. Revised by Nicholas Slonimsky. New York: G. Schirmer, Inc., 1958.

Baldwin, Lillian L. *A Listener's Anthology of Music*. Vol. I, "The Master Builders;" Vol. II, "The Musician As Poet, Painter, and Dramatist." Morristown, New Jersey: Silver Burdett Company, 1958.

Bartholomew, Wilmer T. *Acoustics of Music*. Englewood Cliffs, New Jersey: Prentice-Hall, Inc., 1946.

Barzun, Jacques. *Music in American Life*. Garden City, New York: Doubleday & Co., Inc., 1956.

Bauer, Marion. *Twentieth Century Music*. New York: G. Putnam's Sons, 1947.

Bauer, Marion, and Ethel Peyser. *How Music Grew*. New York: G. Putnam's Sons, 1939.

Beranek, Leo Leroy. *Music, Acoustics, and Architecture*. New York: John Wiley & Sons, Inc., 1962.

Berger, Melvin. *Choral Music in Perspective*. New York: Sam Fox Publishing Company, Inc., 1964.

Bernade, Arthur. *Horns, Strings, and Harmony*. Garden City, New York: Doubleday-Anchor & Co., Inc., 1960.

Bernstein, Martin. *Score Reading*. New York: M. Witmark & Sons, 1947.

209

Biancolli, Louis L. *The Analytical Concert Guide.* (Edited by Louis Biancolli and William S. Mann.) London: Cassell & Co., Ltd., 1957. 1957.

Bockman, Guy, and William J. Starr. *Scored for Listening.* New York: Harcourt, Brace & World, Inc., 1964.

Bodky, Erwin. *The Interpretation of Bach's Keyboard Works.* Cambridge, Massachusetts: Harvard University Press, 1960.

Bonanni, Filippo. *The Showcase of Musical Instruments.* New York: Dover Publications, Inc., 1944.

Bonga, Luigi. *The Meeting of Poetry and Music.* Translated by Elio Gianturco and Clara Rosanti. New York: Merlin Press, 1956.

Britton, Allen P. "Music Education in the Nineteen-Sixties," *Music Educators Journal,* XLVII (June-July, 1961), 23-26.

Bronson, B. H. *Catches and Glees of the Eighteenth Century,* Selected from Appollonian Harmony. Revised edition. Berkeley, California: University of California Press, 1955.

Brown, Calvin S. *Music and Literature: A Comparison of the Arts.* Athens: University of Georgia Press, 1948.

Bruner, Jerome. *The Process of Education.* Cambridge, Massachusetts: Harvard University Press, 1960.

Bulfinch, Thomas. *Mythology of Greece and Rome.* New York: Collier Books, 1962.

Burmeister, Clifford A. "The Role of Music in General Education," *Basic Concepts in Music Education,* Fifty-seventh Yearbook, Part II, National Society for the Study of Education. Chicago: National Society for the Study of Education, 1958, pp. 215-235.

Cannon, Beekman C., Alvin H. Johnson, and William G. Waite. *The Art of Music.* New York: Thomas Y. Crowell Company, 1960.

Carse, Adam. *Musical Wind Instruments.* London: Macmillan Co., 1939. Reprint ed., New York: Da Capo Press, 1965.

Carse, Adam. *The Orchestra from Beethoven to Berlioz.* New York: Broude Bros., 1949.

Carse, Adam. *The Orchestra in the XVIII Cenutry.* New York: Broude Bros., 1950.

Chávez, Carlos. *Towards New Music.* New York: W. W. Norton & Co., Inc., 1937.

Christiansen, Olaf C., and Carol M. Pitts, eds. *The Junior A Cappella Chorus Book.* Bryn Mawr, Pennsylvania: Theodore Presser Company, 1932.

Clough, John. *Scales, Intervals, Keys and Triads.* New York: W. W. Norton & Co., Inc., 1964.

Collins, Walter S. "A selected list of Renaissance and Baroque choral works with sacred English texts in practical editions." *Research Memo No. 22* (March, 1961). New York: American Choral Foundation, Inc.

Conant, James Bryant. *The American High School Today.* New York: McGraw-Hill Book Co., Inc., 1959.

Cooper, Grosvenor, and Leonard B. Meyer. *The Rhythmic Structure of Music.* Chicago: University of Chicago Press, 1960.

Cooper, Irvin, *et al.* "Records by the Billion," *Music in Our Life*. Morristown, New Jersey: Silver Burdett Company, 1959.

Cooper, Irvin, *et al.* "The World of Sound in Hi-Fi," *Music in Our Time*. Morristown, New Jersey: Silver Burdett Company, 1959.

Coover, James, and Richard Colvig. *Medieval and Renaissance Music on Long-Playing Records*. Detroit: Information Service Inc., 1964.

Copland, Aaron. *Music and Imagination*. Cambridge, Massachusetts: Harvard University Press, 1952.

Copland, Aaron. *What To Listen for in Music*. Revised edition. New York: McGraw-Hill Book Co., Inc., 1957.

Corey, Stephen M., *et al. General Education in the American High School*, a sub-committee report of the North Central Association of Colleges and Secondary Schools. Chicago: Scott, Foresman and Co., 1942.

Cotton, Edith M. *Historical Panorama*. Minneapolis: Schmitt, Hall & McCreary Company.

Cronin, Joseph M. "The Principal's Role in Change," *The Bulletin* of the National Association of Secondary School Principals, Vol. 47, No. 283 (May, 1963), 29.

Culver, Charles. *Musical Acoustics*. Fourth edition. New York: McGraw-Hill Book Co., Inc., 1956.

D'Abreu, Gerald. *Playing the Piano with Confidence*. New York: St. Martin's Press, Inc., 1965.

Dart, Thurston. *The Interpretation of Music*. London: Hutchinson & Co., Ltd., 1954. Pocket ed., New York: Harper & Row, Publishers, Inc., 1963.

Davison, Archibald T. *Bach and Handel: The Consummation of the Baroque in Music*. Cambridge, Massachusetts: Harvard University Press, 1951.

Davison, Archibald T., and Willi Apel. *Historical Anthology of Music*. Vols. I and II. Cambridge, Massachusetts: Harvard University Press, 1950.

Dilla, Geraldine P. "Music-Drama: An Art Form in Four Dimensions," *The Musical Quarterly*, X, No. 4 (October, 1924), 492-499.

Doll Edna, and Mary Jarman Nelson. *Rhythms Today*. Morristown, New Jersey: Silver Burdett Company, 1965.

Donington, Robert. *The Instruments of Music*. New York: Barnes & Noble, Inc., 1962.

Donington, Robert. *The Interpretation of Early Music*. New York: St. Martin's Press, Inc., 1964.

Dorf, R. H. *Electronic Musical Instruments*. New York: Radiofile, 1958.

Dunkel, Harold Baker. *General Education in the Humanites*. Washington: The American Council on Education, 1947.

Earhart, Will. *The Meaning and Teaching of Music*. New York: M. Witmark & Sons, 1935.

Eberhart, Constance. "A select list of operas suitable for performance by school groups," *Research Memo No. 45* (December, 1963). New York: American Choral Foundation, Inc.

Ellinwood, Leonard. *The History of American Church Music.* New York: Morehouse-Gorham, 1953.

Engleman, Finis E. "Music and Public Education," *Music Educators Journal,* XLVII (February-March, 1961), 35-39.

Ernst, Karl D. "The General Music Program," *Music Educators Journal,* XLVI (January, 1960), 19-20.

Ernst, Karl D., *et al. Birchard Music Series,* Books Seven and Eight. Evanston, Illinois: Summy-Birchard Company, 1958.

Ewen, David. *American Composers Today.* New York: H. W. Wilson Co., 1949.

Ewen, David. *European Composers Today.* New York: H. W. Wilson Co., 1954.

Farnsworth, Paul R. *The Social Psychology of Music.* New York: Holt, Rinehart & Winston, Inc., 1958.

Ferguson, Donald N. *Masterworks of the Orchestral Repertoire.* Minneapolis: University of Minnesota Press, 1954.

Ferguson, Donald N. *On the Elements of Expression in Music.* Minneapolis: University of Minnesota Press, 1944.

Fiske, Roger. *Score Reading.* Book I, Orchestration; Book II, Musical Form; Book III, Concertos. London: Oxford University Press, 1960.

Fletcher, H. G. "Music Appreciation As an Aid in Band and Orchestra Instruction," *Music Educators Journal,* XXIII (November-December, 1944), 24-26.

Fleming, William. *Arts and Ideas.* New York: Henry Holt & Co., 1955.

Fleming, William, and Abraham Veinus. *Understanding Music: Style, Structure, and History.* New York: Henry Holt & Co., 1958.

Gardner, Helen. *Art Through the Ages.* New York: Harcourt, Brace & World, Inc., 1959.

Gary, Charles L. *A Career in Music Education.* Washington: Music Educators National Conference, 1962.

Gary, Charles L. "The Report on General Music," *Music Educators Journal,* XLVI (June-July, 1960), 21-23.

Geiringer, Karl. *The Bach Family: Seven Generations of Creative Genius.* New York: Oxford University Press, 1947.

Geiringer, Karl. *The Music of the Bach Family.* Cambridge, Massachusetts: Harvard University Press, 1951.

Geiringer, Karl. *Musical Instruments: Their History in Western Culture from Stone Age to the Present.* New York: Oxford University Press, Inc., 1945.

Gelatt, Roland. *The Fabulous Phonograph: From Tin Foil to High Fidelity.* Philadelphia: J. B. Lippincott Company, 1955.

Goldman, Richard Franko. *The Wind Band: Its Literature and Technique.* Boston: Allyn and Bacon, Inc., 1961.

Goldstein, Harriet, and Vetta Goldstein. *Art in Everyday Life*. New York: Macmillan Co., 1954.

Green, Douglass M. *Form in Tonal Music*. New York: Holt, Rinehart and Winston, Inc., 1965.

Greenberg, Noah. *An English Songbook*. Garden City, New York: Doubleday & Co., Inc., 1961.

Greenberg, Noah. "A selective list of XV and XVI century Netherlandish choral music available in practical editions," *Research Memo No. 13* (March, 1960). New York: American Choral Foundation, Inc.

Grew, Eva Mary, and Sydney Grew. *Bach*. New York: Farrar, Straus and Co., 1949.

Grout, Donald J. *A History of Western Music*. New York: W. W. Norton & Co., Inc., 1960. Shorter edition, 1964.

Hanschumacher, James R. "Foundations for the Development of a High School Course in Music Literature Based on the Principles of General Education, with Implications for Teacher Education." Unpublished doctoral dissertation, The Ohio State University, 1961.

Hartnoll, Phyllis, ed. *Shakespeare in Music*. Essays by John Stevens, Charles Codworth, Winton Dean, and Roger Fiske. New York: St. Martin's Press, Inc., 1964.

Hartshorn, William C. *Music for the Academically Talented Student*. Washington: Music Educators National Conference, 1960.

Hartshorn, William C. "The Role of Listening," *Basic Concepts in Music Education*. Fifty-seventh Yearbook, Part II, National Society for the Study of Education. Chicago: University of Chicago Press, 1958.

Hartshorn, William C., and Helen S. Leavitt. *Making Friends with Music*. Four volumes and two teacher's books. Boston: Ginn & Co., 1940.

Heffner, H. C. "Theatre and Drama in Liberal Education," *Teachers College Record*, LXVI (January, 1964), 311-317.

Helmholtz, Hermann L. F. *Sensations of Tone*. New York: Dover Publications, Inc., 1954.

Hertz, Wayne S., ed. *Music in the Senior High School*. Washington: Music Educators National Conference, 1959.

Hickok, Robert. "A selective list of Baroque choral works in practical editions," *Research Memo No. 15* (June, 1960). New York: American Choral Foundation, Inc.

Hiller, Lejaren A., and Leonard T. Isaacson. *Experimental Music*. New York: McGraw-Hill Book Co., Inc., 1959.

Hindemith, Paul. *Johann Sebastian Bach: Heritage and Obligation*. New Haven, Connecticut: Yale University Press, 1952.

Hopkins, Anthony. *Talking About Concertos*. Belmont, California: Wadsworth Publishing Company, Inc., 1964.

Hopkins, Anthony. *Talking About Symphonies*. Belmont, California: Wadsworth Publishing Company, Inc., 1961.

House, Robert. "The Role of the Fine Arts in the Preparation of Teachers," *Music Educators Journal*, XLVII (November-December, 1960), 39-43.

The Hymnal 1940 Companion. New York: Protestant Episcopal Church in the U.S.A., 1951.

Indiana Department of Public Instruction. *Music in Indiana.* Indianapolis: The Department, 1963.

Jacobs, Arthur, ed. *Choral Music.* Baltimore: Penguin Books, 1963.

Kerman, Joseph. "The Place of Music in Basic Education," *Music Educators Journal,* XLVI (April-May, 1960), 43-46.

Keyboard Jr. 8 times a year. New Haven, Connecticut: Keyboard Jr. Publications, Inc.

Kinney, Bik. "Experiments in Sound and Music," *Keyboard Jr.* (October, 1964), 4.

Kinsky, George, and others. *History of Music in Pictures.* Reprint. New York: Dover Publications, Inc., 1951.

Kirby, Percival Robson. *The Kettle-Drums.* New York: Oxford University Press, 1930.

Kristeller, Paul Oskar. *The Philosophy of Marsilio Ficino.* Translated by Virginia Conant. New York: Columbia University Press, 1943.

Krone, Max. *Expressive Conducting.* Park Ridge, Illinois: Neil A. Kjos Music Co., 1945.

Krueger, Karl. *The Way of the Conductor: His Origins, Purposes, and Procedures.* New York: Charles Scribner's Sons, 1958.

Landeck, Beatrice. "Basic Ideas in Elementary Music," *Music Educators Journal* (February-March, 1964), 67-70.

Lang, Paul Henry. *Music in Western Civilization.* New York: W. W. Norton & Co., Inc., 1941.

La Rue, Jan, and John Vinton. "A selective list of choral compositions from the classical period in practical editions," *Research Memo No. 24* (June, 1961). New York: American Choral Foundation, Inc.

Leichentritt, Hugo. *Music, History, and Ideas.* Cambridge, Massachusetts: Harvard University Press, 1938.

Let's Explore Music. Set of 13 papers. Toronto, Ontario: Gordon V. Thompson, Ltd.

Lippman, Edward A. *Musical Thought in Ancient Greece.* New York: Columbia University Press, 1965.

Lowery, H. *A Guide to Musical Acoustics.* London: Dennis Dobson, 1956.

McGehee, Thomasine. *People and Music.* Revised in 1964 by Alice D. Nelson. Boston: Allyn and Bacon, Inc., 1939, 1964.

McGinn, Donald J., and George Howerton, eds. *Literature As a Fine Art.* Evanston, Illinois: Row Peterson and Company, 1959.

McGrath, Earl J., *et al. Toward General Education.* New York: Macmillan Co., 1948.

McKinney, Howard D., and W. R. Anderson. *Discovering Music.* Third edition. New York: American Book Co., 1948.

Machlis, Joseph. *Introduction to Contemporary Music.* New York: W. W. Norton & Co., Inc., 1961.

May, Elizabeth. "The Influence of the Meiji Period on Japanese Children's Music," *Journal of Research in Music Education,* XIII (Summer, 1965).

Mayhew, Lewis B. *General Education: An Account and Appraisal.* New York: Harper and Brothers, 1940.

Meyer, Leonard B. *Emotion and Meaning in Music.* Chicago: University of Chicago Press, 1956.

Meyer, Max. *How We Hear: How Tones Make Music.* Newton Centre, Massachusetts: Charles T. Branford Co., 1950.

Missouri State Department of Education. *The Allied Arts, A High School Humanities Guide.* Jefferson City, Missouri: The Department, 1963.

Modisett, Katherine Carpenter. "Bibliography of Sources, 1930-1952, Relating to the Teaching of Choral Music in Secondary Schools," *Journal of Research in Music Education,* III (Spring, 1955), 51-60.

Montgomery, E. R. *The Story Behind Musical Instruments.* New York: Dodd, Mead & Co., 1953.

Moore, Christopher. "A bibliography of contemporary choral music for high voices performable by children," *Research Memo No. 36* (December 1962). New York: American Choral Foundation, Inc.

Morie, Wayne. "Principal Instrumental Forms of the Baroque Era," *Missouri Journal of Research in Music Education,* I (Autumn, 1962), 46-49.

Mueller, John H. *The American Symphony Orchestra.* Bloomington, Indiana: Indiana University Press, 1951.

Mursell, James L. *Music Education: Principles and Programs.* Morristown, New Jersey: Silver Burdett Company, 1956.

Mursell, James L. *The Psychology of Music.* New York: W. W. Norton & Co., Inc., 1937.

Music Educators National Conference. *Materials for Miscellaneous Instrumental Ensembles.* Washington: Music Educators National Conference, 1960.

Music Educators National Conference. *Music Buildings, Rooms and Equipment.* Washington: Music Educators National Conference, 1955.

Music Research Foundation. *Music and Your Emotions.* New York: Liveright Publishing Corporation, 1952.

Myers, Bernard S. *Understanding the Arts.* New York: Henry Holt & Co., 1958.

National Association of Secondary School Principals. "The Arts in the Comprehensive High School," *The Bulletin,* September 1962. (See also the *Music Educators Journal,* XLVIII, (November-December, 1962), 60-66.

National Interscholastic Music Activities Commission. *Selective Music Lists; Choral, String Orchestra, Orchestra, Band.* Washington: Music Educators National Conference, 1964.

National Interscholastic Music Activities Commission. *Selective Music Lists; Instrumental and Vocal Solos and Ensembles.* Washington: Music Educators National Conference, 1963.

National Society for the Study of Education. *General Education.* Fifty-first Yearbook, Part I. Chicago: University of Chicago Press, 1952.

Nettl, Bruno. *An Introduction to Folk Music in the United States.* Detroit: Wayne State University Press, 1960.

Nettl, Paul. *The Dance in Classical Music.* New York: Philosophical Library, Inc., 1963.

Newman, Ernest. *Stories of Great Operas.* New York: Garden City Books, 1950.

Newman, Ernest. *The Wagner Operas.* New York: Alfred A. Knopf, 1949.

Newman, William S. *The Sonata in The Baroque Era.* Chapel Hill: University of North Carolina Press, 1959.

Newman, William S. *The Sonata in The Classic Era.* Chapel Hill: University of North Carolina Press, 1963.

North Carolina Department of Public Instruction. *Consumer Music for High Schools.* Raleigh: The Department (Pub. No. 367), 1963.

Opera News. New York: Metropolitan Opera Guild.

Parrish, Carl, and John F. Ohl. *Masterpieces of Music Before 1750.* New York: W. W. Norton & Co., Inc., 1951.

Pater, Walter. *The Renaissance.* Cleveland: World Publishing Co. (Meridian Books), 1961.

Pincherle, Marc. *An Illustrated History of Music.* Edited by George and Rosamund Bornier. New York: William Morrow and Co., Inc., (Reynal & Co., Inc.), 1959.

Porter, Harold B. "An Integrated Course in Music Literature, Theory, and Ensemble Performance for Talented High School Students." Unpublished doctoral dissertation, University of Arizona, 1964.

Portland Public Schools. *A Course in the Understanding of Music.* Portland: Portland Public Schools, 1961.

Portnoy, Julius. *Music in the Life of Man.* New York: Holt, Rinehart & Winston, Inc., 1963.

Portnoy, Julius. *The Philosopher and Music.* New York: The Humanities Press, 1954.

Rader, Melvin. *A Modern Book of Esthetics.* New York: Holt, Rinehart & Winston, Inc., 1960.

Rafferty, Sadie, and Nick Rossi. *Music Through the Centuries.* Boston: Bruce Humphries Publishers, 1964.

Randolph, David. *This Is Music.* New York: McGraw-Hill Book Co., Inc., 1964.

Read, Gardner. *Music Notation: A Manual of Modern Practices.* Boston: Allyn and Bacon, Inc., 1964.

Read, Oliver, and Walter L. Welch. *From Tin Foil to Stereo: Evolution of the Phonograph.* Indianapolis: Howard W. Sams & Co., 1959.

The Record Hunter. Institutional Order Book for Long Playing Records. New York: The Record Hunter, 1963.

Rensin, Hy. *Basic Course in Music*. New York: Edwin H. Morris & Company, Inc., 1955.

Revesz, G. *Introduction to the Psychology of Music*. Translated by G. I. C. de Courcy. Norman, Oklahoma: University of Oklahoma Press, 1954.

Richardson, Allen L., and Mary E. English. *Living with Music*. Vols. I and II. New York: M. Witmark & Sons, 1958.

Richardson, E. G. *The Acoustics of Orchestral Instruments and of the Organ*. London: Edward Arnold & Co., 1929.

Robbins, Rossell Hope. *Early English Christmas Carols*. New York: Columbia University Press, 1961.

Routly, Eric. *The English Carol*. New York: Oxford University Press, 1959.

Rubsamen, Walter H. "Melody" *The International Cyclopedia of Music and Musicians*. Ninth edition. New York: Dodd Mead & Company, 1964.

Rudolf, Max. *The Grammar of Conducting*. New York: G. Schirmer, Inc., 1950.

Sachs, Curt. *The Commonwealth of Art*. New York: W. W. Norton & Co., Inc., 1946.

Sachs, Curt. *The History of Musical Instruments*. New York: W. W. Norton & Co., Inc., 1940.

Sachs, Curt. *Rhythm and Tempo*. New York: W. W. Norton & Co., Inc., 1953.

Salazar, Adolfo. *Music in Our Time*. New York: W. W. Norton & Co., Inc., 1946.

Sargent, Malcolm, editor. *The Outline of Music*. New York: Arco Publishing Co., 1963.

Schoen, Max. *Art and Beauty*. Riverside, New Jersey: Macmillan Co., 1932.

Schoen, Max. *The Understanding of Music*. New York: Harper and Bros., 1945.

Scholes, Percy A., ed. *The Oxford Companion to Music*. New York: Oxford University Press, 1955.

Schweitzer, Albert. *J. S. Bach* (2 vols.) Boston: Bruce Humphries, Publishers, 1964.

Seashore, Carl E. *In Search of Beauty in Music*. New York: Ronald Press, 1947.

Serposs, Emile, and Ira Singleton. *Music In Our Heritage*. Morristown, New Jersey: Silver Burdett Company, 1963.

Sessions, Roger. *Reflections on Musical Life in the U. S.* New York: Merlin Press, 1956.

Sexton, Ada Jeanette. "Music in General Education." Unpublished doctoral dissertation, Michigan State University, 1963.

Shemel, Sidney, and M. William Krasilovsky. *This Business of Music.* Edited by Paul Ackerman. New York: Billboard Publishing Company, 1964.

Shetler, Donald J. *Film Guide for Music Educators.* Washington: Music Educators National Conference, 1961.

Small, Terrence S. "The Use of Oscilloscopic Transparencies as a Diagnostic Tool in the Evaluation of Clarinet Tone Quality." Unpublished dissertation, Western Reserve University, 1964.

Smith, Cecil. *Worlds of Music.* Philadelphia: J. B. Lippincott Co., 1952.

Starr, William J., and George F. Devine. *Music Scores Omnibus.* Parts I and II. Englewood Cliffs, New Jersey. Prentice-Hall, Inc., 1964.

Stringham, Edwin J. *Listening to Music Creatively.* Englewood Cliffs, New Jersey: Prentice-Hall, Inc., 1959.

Sur, William R. "Music for Teenagers," *Music Educators Journal,* XLVII (November-December, 1960), 62-68.

Sur, William R., and Charles Francis Schuller. *Music for Teenagers.* New York: Harper and Brothers, 1958.

Terry, Charles Sanford. *Bach: A Biography.* New York: Oxford University Press, 1933.

Terry, Charles Sanford. *Bach's Orchestra.* New York: Oxford University Press, 1958.

Terry, Charles Sanford. *The Music of Bach.* New York: Dover Publications, Inc., 1963.

Toch, Ernst. *The Shaping Forces of Music.* New York: Criterion Music Corporation, 1948.

Toffler, Alvin. *The Culture Consumers.* New York: St. Martin's Press, 1964.

Tovey, Donald Francis. *Essays in Musical Analysis.* Vol. 1, Symphonies; Vol. 2, Symphonies; Vol. 3, Concertos; Vol. 4, Illustrative Music—1956 edition; Vol. 5, Vocal Music—1956 edition; Vol. 6, Miscellaneous Notes—1957 edition. New York: Oxford University Press.

Trump, J. Lloyd, and Dorsey Baynham. *Focus on Change.* Chicago: Rand McNally & Company, 1961.

Ulrich, Homer. *Chamber Music.* New York: Columbia University Press, 1948.

Ulrich, Homer. *Symphonic Music.* New York: Columbia University Press, 1952.

Ulrich, Homer, and Paul A. Pisk. *A History of Music and Musical Style.* New York: Harcourt, Brace and World, Inc., 1963.

United States Information Agency. *Catalog of Published Concert Music by American Composers.* Washington: U. S. Government Printing Office, 1964.

Wagoner, William H. *Staff Development—An Emerging Function For Schools*. Washington: National Education Association, Department of Rural Education, 1964.

Walter, Bruno. *Of Music and Music Making*. New York: W. W. Norton & Co., Inc., 1961.

Wold, Milo A., and Edmund Cykler. *Introduction to Music and Art in the Western World*. Dubuque: W. C. Brown Co., 1955.

Wood, Alexander. *The Physics of Music*. New York: Dover Publications, Inc., 1944.

Young, Percy M. *The Choral Tradition*. New York: W. W. Norton & Co., Inc., 1962.

Young, Percy M. *Instrumental Music*. London: Methven & Co., Ltd., 1958.

Directory of Publishers

Am.Comp.All.—American Composers Alliance, 2121 Broadway, New York City 10023

Ashley Dealers Service, 39 West 60th Street, New York City 10023

Associated Music Publishers, Inc., 609 Fifth Avenue, New York City 10017

Berkeley Publishing Co., 2244 Dwight Way, Berkeley, California 94704

Berlin, Irving, 1290 Avenue of the Americas, New York City 10019

Big Three Music Corp., 1540 Broadway, New York City 10036

Boosey & Hawkes, Inc., Oceanside, New York 11572

Boston Music Co., 116 Boylston Street, Boston 02116

Bourne, Inc., 136 West 52nd Street, New York City 10019

British American—See Brodt

Broadcast Music, Inc., 589 Fifth Avenue, New York City 10017

Brodt Music Co., P. O. Box 1207, Charlotte, North Carolina 28201

Broude Bros., 56 West 45th Street, New York City 10036

Carlin Music Co., Oakhurst, California 93644

Century—See Ashley

Chappell & Co., Inc., 609 Fifth Avenue, New York City 10017

Choral Art—See Fox

Colombo, Inc., Franco, 16 West 61st Street, New York City 10023

Concordia Publishing House, 3558 S. Jefferson Avenue, St. Louis, Missouri 63118

Ditson—See Presser

Doubleday Co., 501 Franklin Avenue, Garden City, L. I., New York 11040

Elkan Music Publishers, Henri, 1316 Walnut Street, Philadelphia 19107

Elkan-Vogel Co., Inc., 1712-16 Sansom Street, Philadelphia 19103

Elkin & Co.—See Galaxy

Fischer, Inc., Carl, 62 Cooper Square, New York City 10003

Fischer & Bro., J., Harristown Road, Glen Rock, New Jersey 07452

FitzSimons Co., H. T., 615 North La Salle Street, Chicago 60610

Flammer, Inc., Harold, 251 West 19th Street, New York City 10011

Fox Music Pub. Co., Sam, 11 West 60th Street, New York City 10023

Galaxy Music Corp., 2121 Broadway, New York City 10023

Gillman Publications, Box 8671, Crenshaw Station, Los Angeles 90056

Gray Co., Inc., H. W., 159 East 48th Street, New York City 10017

Hansen Publications, Inc., 1814 West Avenue, Miami Beach, Florida 33139

Hargail Music, Inc., 157 West 57th Street, New York City 10019

Hoffman, Raymond A., 1421 Coolidge Avenue, Wichita, Kansas 67203

International Music Co., 509 Fifth Ave., New York City 10017

Kalmus, Edwin F., P.O. Box 47, Huntington Station, L.I., New York 11744

King Music Co., Robert, 7 Canton Street, North Easton, Massachusetts 02356

Kjos Music Co., Neil A., 525 Busse Highway, Park Ridge, Illinois 60068

Lawson-Gould Music Publishers, Inc., 609 Fifth Avenue, New York City 10036

Leeds Music Corp., 322 West 48th Street, New York City 10036

Ludwig Music Publishing Co., 557 East 140th Street, Cleveland 44110

Marks Music Corp., Edward B., 136 West 52nd Street, New York City 10019

Mercury—See Presser

Merion—See Presser

Mills Music, Inc., 1619 Broadway, New York City 10019

MPHC—Music Publishers Holding Corp., 619 West 54th Street, New York City 10019

Novello—See Gray

Oxford University Press, Inc., 417 Fifth Avenue, New York City 10016

Peer Int.—See Southern Music Publishing Co.

Peters Corp., C. F., 373 Park Avenue South, New York City 10016

Plymouth Music Co., Inc., 1841 Broadway, New York City 10023

Presser Co., Theodore, Presser Place, Bryn Mawr, Pennsylvania 19010

Pro Art Publications, 469 Union Avenue, Westbury, New York 11591

Record Hunter, The, 507 Fifth Avenue, New York City 10017

Remick—See MPHC

Ricordi—See Colombo

Robbins—See Big Three

Rubank, Inc., 5544 West Armstrong Avenue, Chicago 60646

Schirmer, E. C., 600 Washington Street, Boston 02111

Schirmer, Inc., G., 609 Fifth Avenue, New York City 10017

SHM—Schmitt, Hall and McCreary Co., 527 Park Avenue, Minneapolis 55415

Schott—See Associated

Shapiro, Bernstein & Co., Inc., 666 Fifth Avenue, New York City 10019

Shawnee Press, Inc., Delaware Water Gap, Pennsylvania 18327

Skidmore—See Shapiro, Bernstein & Co.

So.Mus.Pub.Co.—Southern Music Publishing Co., Inc., 1619 Broadway, New York City 10019

Spratt Music Co., Jack, 77 West Broad Street, Stamford, Connecticut 06901

Staff Music Publishing Co., 374 Great Neck Road, Great Neck, New York 11021

Summy-Birchard Co., 1834 Ridge Avenue, Evanston, Illinois 60204

Transcontinental Music Corp., 1674 Broadway, New York City 10019

University of California Press, Berkeley, California 94704

Witmark—See MPHC

Wood—See Mills

Wynn Music Publications, 1511 McGee, Berkeley, California 94703

Directory of Film Producers

Almanac—Almanac Films Inc., 41 Union Square W., New York City 10003

Ambrosch—Harold Ambrosch Film Productions, Box 98, Glendale, California 91205

Association—Association Films, Inc., 347 Madison Avenue, New York City 10017

Avis—Avis Films, P.O. Box 643, Burbank, California 91503

Baldwin—Baldwin Piano Co., Advertising Dept., 1801 Gilbert Avenue, Cincinnati 45202

Bell Tel—Bell Telephone System (apply local office) or American Telephone and Telegraph Co., Motion Picture Section, 195 Broadway, New York City 10007

Bowmar—Bowmar Co., Inc., Stanley, 12 Cleveland Street, Valhalla, New York 10595

Brandon—Brandon Films Inc., 200 West 57th Street, New York City 10019

Conn—C. G. Conn, Ltd., Educational Services Dept., Elkhart, Indiana 46514

Contemporary—Contemporary Films, Inc., 267 West 25th Street, New York City 10001

Coronet—Coronet Instructional Films, Coronet Bldg., 65 East South Water Street, Chicago 60601

EBF—Encyclopaedia Britannica Films, Inc., 1150 Wilmette Avenue, Wilmette, Illinois 60091

Film Images—Film Images, Inc., 1860 Broadway, New York City 10023

Films of Nations—Films of the Nations Distributors, Inc., 62 West 45th Street, New York City 10036

Florida—University Broadcasting Services, The Florida State University, Tallahassee, Florida 32306

Hammond—Hammond Organ Co., Advertising Dept., 4200 West Diversey Avenue, Chicago 60639

Harmon—Harmon Foundation Inc., 140 Nassau Street, New York City 10038

Hoffberg—Hoffberg Productions Inc., 362 West 44th Street, New York City 10018

IFB—International Film Bureau, Inc., 332 South Michigan Avenue, Chicago 60604

IVT—Institute of Visual Training, 40 East 49th Street, New York City 10017

India—Consulate General of India, 417 Montgomery Street, San Francisco 94104

Indiana—Indiana University, Audio-Visual Center, Bloomington, Indiana 47405

Iowa State—Iowa State University, Visual Instruction Service, Ames, Iowa 50012

Jam Handy—Jam Handy Organization, 2821 East Grand Blvd., Detroit 48211

Mahnke—Carl F. Mahnke Productions, 215 East 3rd Street, Des Moines 50309

McGraw-Hill—McGraw-Hill Book Co., Inc., Text-Film Dept., 330 West 42nd Street, New York City 10018

Modern—Modern Learning Aids, 3 East 54th Street, New York City 10022

NET—NET Film Service, Indiana University, Audio-Visual Center, Bloomington, Indiana 47405

NFBC—National Film Board of Canada, 680 Fifth Avenue, New York City 10019

Pictura—Pictura Films Distribution Corp., 41 Union Square, New York City 10003

Rembrandt—Rembrandt Films, 15 East 48th Street, New York City 10017

UMTV—University of Michigan TV, 310 Maynard Street, Ann Arbor, Michigan 48108

UW—United World Films, Inc., 1445 Park Avenue, New York City 10029